Design Adventures

Discover a Creative Framework for Effective Change

Looby Macnamara

permanent publications

Published by
Permanent Publications
Hyden House Ltd
13 Clovelly Road
Portsmouth
PO4 8DL
United Kingdom
Tel: 01730 776 582
Email: enquiries@permaculture.co.uk
Web: www.permanentpublications.co.uk

Distributed in North America by Chelsea Green Publishing Company, PO Box 428, White River Junction, VT 05001, USA www.chelseagreen.com

Distributed in Australia by Peribo Pty Limited, 58 Beaumont Road, Mt Kuring-Gai, NSW 2080 Australia https://peribo.com.au

Designed by Two Plus George Limited, info@twoplusgeorge.co.uk

Printed in the UK by SRP Ltd, Bittern Road, Sowton Industrial Estate, Exeter EX2 7LW

FSC www.fsc.org MIX Paper | Supporting responsible forestry FSC® C014540

This product is made of material from well-managed FSC®-certified forests and from recycled materials and other controlled sources.

The Forest Stewardship Council ® (FSC) is a non-profit international organisation established to promote the responsible management of the world's forests. Products carrying the FSC label are independently certified to assure consumers that they come from forests that are managed to meet the social, economic and ecological needs of present and future generations.

British Library Cataloguing-in-Publication Data
A catalogue record for this book is available from the British Library

ISBN 978 1 85623 203 6

Praise for the book

Design Adventures is a visionary, inspiring book for our times: nobody else is going to lead us forward to a future we'd be proud to leave behind: it's down to us now, each of us to embrace our potential and offer ourselves in service to life. And what we need along the way is a beautifully crafted, heart-full guide that we can dive into and know there is wonder in the heart of permaculture, in the world, in ourselves. We can do this, all of us. And Looby's book will lead the way.

Manda Scott,
Podcaster, author and thrutopian writer

Looby Macnamara sheds fresh light on the sensing, feeling and thinking necessary to generate effective and positive change. Her Design Web is a useful template to help us organise that most mysterious and chaotic part of permaculture; the design process.

Dr David Holmgren,
Permaculture co-originator on Dja Dja Wurrung Country

Design Adventures is an indispensable guide for leading positive change in the world – the micro to the macro, from personal to the political. Looby's way of describing design is liberating and enticingly accessible, and her wonderful tools help us to unleash our imagination and manifest good things for both people and the planet. A new permaculture classic is born.

Morag Gamble Founder,
Permaculture Education Institute

The Design Web is an incredible visionary tool. Looby has brought forth this brilliant offering and made the path visible, inspiring and graceful through *Design Adventures*. I have been working with Design Web since meeting Looby in 2016 and this process has literally transformed my life, the lives of many colleagues and collaborators, and has changed how I bring my own work to serve in significant and powerfully effective ways. The magic inherent in this important approach can, and will, change the world for the better!

Jon Young,
Author, storyteller, teacher and Founder of Living Connection 1st

Design Adventures is a valuable resource for designing everything from a garden to a life transition. I look forward to using it in my permaculture courses, and for myself! Looby draws on her own rich experience to provide a gift for all of us.

Starhawk,
Author, activist, permaculture designer and teacher

Looby has made design and the whole process of change, exciting, accessible and yes, enjoyable and liberating! Packed with principles, tools, processes and flows, case studies and a wealth of questions and activities that can help you get started, this book is an enormous gift to everyone that wants to help create a better world. Thanks Looby!

Andy Goldring,
Permaculture Britain CEO, permaculture teacher and designer

I congratulate Looby on yet another book to join those she has already contributed to in the permaculture library.

Rosemary Morrow,
Permaculture author and teacher

Wow! What a wonderfully helpful guide for inspiring and supporting any adventure, be it your own personal lifestyle or health journey, a community co-creation, your land design, neighbourhood renewal or a retrofit of our world systems! Looby's Cultural Emergence framework and use of permaculture design inform this much needed book and her care, compassion, creativity and brilliant design thinking is now available to inspire us all. Enjoy the journey.

Robin Clayfield,
Permaculture elder, social permaculture 'Grandmother',
bestselling author and creative education facilitator

I am quite sure that Looby wrote *Design Adventures* specifically for me. At least that is how relatable her inspiring words, thoughtful questions, brilliant storytelling, and examples are. I can use this! From simple to complex; doable in mini successes to harvests of magnitude. I will use the wisdom of this book while designing full systems for my personal life to connections with others and the communities we live in.

Becky Wilson,
Co-founder of Midwest Permaculture

If you struggle to vision or execute change large or small, then this book, the latest by legendary permaculturalist Looby Macnamara, may be for you. It is a kind of handbook for thrutopian design, full of vital and often initially counter-intuitive suggestions, such as the profound importance of pausing if you want to get things done, or the possibility of co-creating the seemingly impossible: if you are able to trust the process.

Emeritus Prof. Rupert Read,
Editor of *Transformative Adaptation* and Co-director of the Climate Majority Project

We need more heart-centred design processes like these! This book feels like a warm hug, while also holding you firm on the ground, rooted and connected with each other. The worlds our communities need and deserve will emerge from design adventures like these.

Kirsten Bradley (she/her),
Milkwood.net

Just as every seasoned backpacker learns to carry a multi-tool, every designer needs a flexible design framework they can carry with them and apply to any situation. The Design Web can be applied to positively transform every aspect of one's life and world, at any scale, individually or with others. It is sturdy and time-tested. And thanks to Looby's warm and wise guidance, it is easy for anyone to access and use.

Don Hall,
Training Coordinator for the international Transition Network
and author of *The Regeneration Handbook*

Design Adventures oozes with the kind of wisdom and joy that are signs of true mastery. With clear advice and easy to follow prompts and activities that include planning and mapping as well as creative practice, embodiment and wisdom from nature, this book offers a wonderfully accessible approach to shifting the way we go about creating the lives we want. This is a truly transformative tool for liberating the power to shape our lives, as individuals, communities, and members of the wider web of life. I will be recommending to everyone I know, and look forward to integrating the Design Web more fully into my own life.

Anna Kovasna,
Resilience lead at Global Ecovillage Network;
Co-founder of Kincentric Leadership

Contents

Appreciations

As always there are many people involved with the creation of this book, both directly and indirectly. I am grateful to Jon Young for the co-creation and evolution of Cultural Emergence. I appreciate all the people who are involved in Cultural Emergence and have used the Design Web and shared their stories. Thanks to Delvin Solkinson for co-facilitating the Group Diploma Adventure with me. Gratitude to Emma Gorbutt and Barbara Scheltus for many layers of collaboration, including on the Cultural Emergence collective.

I am grateful for the Permanent Publications team: Maddy Harland, Rozie Apps, Nicola Willmot and Tony Rollinson for all their extensive experience, attention to detail and commitment to sharing regenerative tools. Everlasting gratitude to Tim Harland, although not here on the physical plane for the creation of this book, there is an enduring imprint of his wisdom from previous projects.

Gratitude to the permaculture movement for all the community, co-creation and inspiration. Thank you to all the lineages of teachers that have fed into this book.

Gratitude to all the musicians for accompanying my writing. Deep gratitude to my home, Applewood Permaculture Centre, for holding me and sharing the deep wisdom from the more-than-human world, in particular my cats and dog.

Gratitude to my dad, Tom Macnamara, for his valuable editing advice, and to my mum, Thereza Macnamara, for all her kindness and support.

Everlasting gratitude to my partner, Chris Evans, for all the Design Adventures we have been on together, for sharing my life's journey, and for doing so many early mornings enabling me to write in my own rhythm. Gratitude to my children, Shanti and Teya, for your adventurous spirits.

About the author

Looby Macnamara is an author, designer, gardener, song leader, mother, and artist. She is the author of four influential books: *People & Permaculture, 7 Ways to Think Differently, Cultural Emergence,* and *Strands of Infinity,* and creator of the CEED – Cultural Emergence Empowerment & Design card deck. She is a regular contributor to *Permaculture* magazine and *Earth Pathways* diary.

Looby is a visionary thought leader who inspires thousands with her creative approaches to regenerative change. *People & Permaculture* is the first book globally to translate permaculture to people based systems. Looby is the co-founder of the global Cultural Emergence movement.

For over 20 years, she has been a pioneering teacher. She lives with her partner, Chris Evans, two children, Shanti and Teya, and cats and dog at Applewood Permaculture Centre, a 20-acre smallholding and teaching and demonstration site in Herefordshire, UK. Here she grows food, connects with the wonderful wildlife and hosts people from around the world. She offers Cultural Emergence and Permaculture courses, teacher training and other specialist courses; globally, online and at Applewood. Looby has a passion for creative teaching methods and enjoys inventing participatory activities and games to enhance learning and self-discovery.

She has a degree in Human Sciences, providing a wealth of perspectives to bring into her teaching and writing, and is on the expert panel of the Design Council. Looby is one of the partners of the international Mother Nature project, empowering mothers as natural leaders.

Looby has supported the development and growth of permaculture nationally through her input as trustee of the Permaculture Association (Britain) for five years (2001-2006) and was Chairperson for two of these. She is still an active member of the permaculture community and is a senior diploma tutor.

Foreword

I first 'met' the Design Web in Looby's first book, *People & Permaculture* (2012). Permaculture is a design system with ethics and principles that is firmly rooted in ways of caring for the Earth. Looby wanted to explore how we can elevate 'people care' to have equal value in our designs. The Design Web, for me, is a powerful way of designing effective change in our relationships with ourselves, with people around us, within organisations large and small, and ultimately with culture. It has very clear steps that can be quick to grasp yet, like all brilliant ideas, is subtle and has an elegant simplicity. I realised immediately with *People & Permaculture* that Looby had created something easy to understand and effective that I started using it myself along with many others around the world.

I facilitated a day with a charity that was struggling and needed to unify its staff and trustee volunteers, and develop a shared vision, collective enthusiasm and agency. The Design Web helped us to do all of this and design a plan of action together. The day was a pleasure rather than a chore because it was held by an understandable and clear structure and yet called on all the participants to engage and be creative together.

I have also used the Design Web to clarify the next steps needed in my life with my partner. We wanted to move away from our family home and both needed to find our dream place. Ultimately, having identified what we were both searching for and having created a step by step plan of action, we left our home of 34 years and started a woodland project which has brought great joy and new learnings.

Then came *Cultural Emergence* (2020), Looby's next big book, which offers a toolkit for designing peaceful, regenerative cultures. It sparked a global community that anyone can join, where people meet and share how we are weaving webs of well being, coherence and power to become the best people that we can. Ultimately, the aim is to build a vision and pathways to more wholesome, healing and generative cultures. We do not just want to focus on our own lives, we want to create a more stable, peaceful and abundant world. We start with our personal lives, in our families, our friendships, our communities and enterprises, crafting a mosaic of active peacemaking, each having a role to play in making small islands of coherence that ultimately result in a powerful movement in many countries.

As a complement to this outstanding work, I encouraged Looby to return to the Design Web and explore how it has evolved, both in her work, and within its international community of practitioners. The arising designs can be small yet significant ways of releasing negative self-limiting habits and help us move into more creative, freer ways of being. They can also be life-changing shifts with distinct gear changes, and bigger, shared community projects. It has been exciting and inspiring to watch the adoption of the Design Web seeding around the world, and hearing the many creative ways in which the tools are utilised.

Whilst writing this book, Looby came to stay with me at my new home in a woodland sanctuary. The first thing we did was to design our week together, putting the processes and principles that will inspire you in this book into practice. To live the work so tangibly made our experience energised and productive. We cooked together, drew together, designed together and talked through the creative process, placing flesh on the bones. We also spent time quietly in a special part of the wood to envision what the world will look like when enough people adopt the Design Web and use it in their lives. This is a beautiful and peaceful world where human beings and Nature are able to live together harmoniously; a world where the climate can stabilise, and where finite resources can be shared fairly. During this time, each night, a young tawny owl came from the wood to the edge of the garden and called out, it seemed, to us. We both felt deeply connected to the wild and I am sure this experience and others invited more liminal and creative energies into the making of this book.

Many Indigenous cultures speak of the Spider, a Creator who is able to weave 'reality' from its very core into a Web of Being. We learn that our whole world is created in a web of interconnection akin to a giant spider's web. The Spider Creator Being (often Spiderwoman but not always female) is a protector, a creatrix of worlds, and a healer. In western philosophy, there are teachings of our capacity to build 'bridges' between ourselves and the more-than-human world, and from individual conscious to unity consciousness. These bridges are built from within us, by our intentions and actions, just as the spider weaves a web from the centre of its body.

This may seem intangible but have you ever gone to bed with a problem and woken up with a solution? I often do! Imagine having a waking framework with which to support this problem solving and visioning. This is essentially what the Design Web is. So I invite you to go on a design adventure, using the tools and experiences contained here, to support yourself in realising your dreams. You may want to start with the small patterns you want to shift or design projects with your family, and with colleagues and people you collaborate with in your community. You will find plenty of examples and inspiration here. After some small successes, we hope that you will dare to design a pathway to realising your deepest dreams for the world! So much of what stops us dreaming are self-limiting concepts. The Design Web will help you to overcome the ones that are mutable. Above all, please have fun with it. Wishing you a very warm welcome to the emergent Design Web community.

Maddy Harland
Author of *Fertile Edges – regenerating land, culture & hope*
Editor and Co-founder of *Permaculture* magazine and Permanent Publications

Part 1

Activating our inner designer

Embrace potential

Introduction

Dear Reader,

Welcome to this adventure; individually and collectively adventuring into life, into our gifts, our purpose and visionary leadership. What you have in your hands is a manual full of potential – your potential – for well being, growth, expansion, effectiveness, for taking agency over your life and contributing your gifts into the world. It is brimming with possibilities for joyful, smooth and creative collaborations with friends, family, groups and in the workplace. Full of opportunities for significantly growing the ethics of Earth care, people care and fair shares; expanding our collective circles of care and influence, so that humanity can live in thriving relationship with ourselves and the rest of the web of life.

What is the potential you want to open your arms to? What visions do you want to nurture?

Here, you will discover the Design Web, a framework you can use to design literally anything. You will be able to create captivating designs that balance achievability and ambition. In 2011, while writing my first book, *People & Permaculture*, I went on a quest to find an acronym for a design framework. In the search to find ways to guide people through the multilayered process of manifestation, I played, visioned, and reflected. Instead of a linear acronym, the Design Web was birthed out of this dreaming. Little did I know the rich and varied treasures it would hold. The journey into its creation was a dynamic multilayered sensory experience; I felt into the embodied essence of different stages of the process, I brought in the wisdom of the more-than-human world through watching spiders weave their webs, and woven throughout was the collective intelligence from deep reflections on many permaculture designs and courses.

Since then it has been used by thousands of people around the globe in ways that I couldn't have imagined. From the small and immediate to the large and long term, people have been using the Design Web to support their lives and their projects. It has become a trusted friend for many: ready to listen, advise and help to navigate life.

As humans we have been weaving since time immemorial: weaving for warmth, for protection, for carrying, for holding... Weaving clothes, baskets, blankets, fishing nets, and community. Webs are for catching. The Design Web has caught hope, friendships, purpose, homes, babies, projects, creativity. From tangled threads of confusion, indecision and procrastination, a new and beautiful tapestry of clarity, direction and motivation has emerged.

The Design Web is a fun, easy and doable process that connects with your own inner wisdom, allowing you to weave in your own creativity and life's experience. Design is service, play, joy, alignment, collaboration with life and with all aspects of ourselves. It is an opportunity to step off your endless job list and act with purpose and precision, structure and flexibility.

With the Design Web you travel towards your **vision**; discover both what **helps** and **limits** your movement; observe **patterns** to grow and ones to let go of; engage your imagination to harvest an abundant flow of **ideas**; receive guidance from a set of **principles**; **integrate** your needs and design thinking; plan **action** steps and build **momentum** to manifest and maintain your **vision**; **reflect** to learn lessons from the past to take forward; fuel your journey with **appreciation** and **pause**.

The Design Web is part of the Cultural Emergence toolkit. This toolkit brings together awareness of culture, systems thinking, design and nature connection. The Design Web has grown and redefined itself in relationship and collaboration with these additional tools. The Design Web is part of the Cultural Emergence ecosystem of tools, people, courses, books, card deck, podcasts, networks and online community. The Design Web creates cultures of care, connection, leadership, effectiveness, confidence, peace. It harnesses ways of tending and cultivating personal cultures and methods of co-creating harmonious group cultures.

You will learn how to:

- turn your ideas into reality
- design from the everyday to your wildest dreams
- use nature connection, embodiment and creativity
- integrate the tools of Cultural Emergence
- collaborate and design with others
- make ethical life decisions
- live in alignment.

You will activate and befriend your inner designer through questions, activities, body wisdom, serendipity and synchronicities, through fun and play.

Open your arms to possibilities, relax into emergence, step into the adventure and enjoy!

Pathways through the book

This is a book to participate in. You can start immediately, gaining insights and support. You don't need to think of yourself as a designer, you will grow your skills as you go. The best way to learn is through doing. The more active you are with designing, the more you will gain from reading and the more layers you will understand.

You don't need to travel through page to page, go your own way. I see growth and learning as non-linear processes. One of the feedbacks that I've had from many neurodiverse people is how much they love being able to find their own way in a non-linear fashion with the Design Web. Take it in any direction you want to and become the designer you want to be.

You have travelled many pathways before arriving here. Wherever you are on your journey, you will be bringing a wealth of wisdom and life experience. You might have read some of my other books, participated in courses, and be a designer already. Start small if you are a beginner, and if you are already experienced, use this to enhance, refine and articulate the processes you use.

In this book you will find guides for your week ahead, your health and well being, a culture of effectiveness, events, land and visionary large scale. There is guidance on how to collaborate and co-create with other people. Find the pathways that interest you and are relevant and useful to wherever you are on your journey.

What is design?

Design is an opportunity to create your own path through the wilderness of life and to continually choose and refine decisions. Sometimes it is about getting from A to B, other times it is just about stepping away from A without knowing where we are going, and at times it's about making A a better place to live.

Design is more than just making a plan, it is a holistic process, extending the context to include past and future as well as present, to look below the surface and expand our timeframes, to be realistic and effective. Decision making is enabled with the benefits of multiple perspectives. What is already there is revealed, uncovering important information that guides us forward. It is a dynamic process, creating flow and ease, and balancing flexibility and structure. There is an ongoing journey of discovery. We explore our inner landscapes. Design is the art of asking the right questions, a way of tracking our progress, visions, desires and opportunities. We are embarking on an alchemical process where magic is interwoven with pragmatic thought and decisions.

Stories and design library

Throughout the book you will hear stories from people around the world who have successfully used the Design Web to create positive change in their lives. They are people who have studied with me and are part of the growing community of designers. Here they share insights about different stages of the process and tools.

The online design library is an exciting complement to this book. You can read more about all those featured here, alongside many others. The library shows the breadth and depth of opportunities and the unique creativity that people bring into their designs and ways of presenting them. They will inspire you to experiment and find your own way. Do get involved to help build and share this global collective resource.

Why design?

Designing is a way of manifesting. It allows us to speak our heart's desire, setting intention for change and showing willingness, motivation and commitment. It opens us to possibilities. Many of us have ideas and visions but don't know how to make them real. Design focuses our attention and connects us with our resourcefulness and ability to make things happen.

It is an invitation to change, improve, enhance, fix or start something new. It is used to create products: books, events, websites, organisations, courses. We break out of stuck thinking patterns. It supports us to learn lessons from the past, to let go and move forward with purpose. Through design we become effective change makers.

When collaborating with other people it gives a shared vocabulary, framework, intention and focus. It helps clear the air and brings objectivity, giving some distance between conflicting personalities and agendas. Everyone is invited to be involved and participate, to contribute and co-create. It gives accountability and transparency, and brings a group into alignment with enhanced productivity and cohesion. Therefore design is a tool for peacemaking. Connecting with other change makers exponentially increases our positive impact.

What is a design adventure?

Each time we start, it is a journey into the unknown. When we are planning with plants we are certain that the apple tree is going to give us apples, we might not know when, how many we will get or how sweet they will be, but if it gives us plums, well... we know the labels must have been wrong. When collaborating with people though, anything can happen. The idea of adventure is subverting notions of design being formulaic, precise and having all the answers. Design is a weaving with the mystery of life and our own skills, passions and motivations. It is an opportunity to create our own stories.

We don't know where we will end up, or what surprises and challenges will happen on the way. Stepping into an adventure can be both an exciting and daunting journey of change. These can be unexpected and eventful. There is a pulse between inner discovery and outer movement. It is as much about the process and the path as the destination. Life becomes a series of design adventures.

You are already a designer

Many of us do not think of ourselves as designers. We think that we need specific training to become one. I disagree. I think we all have ways of navigating life on a daily basis that involve these skills. Some everyday examples are cooking a meal, making a journey, inviting friends over, arranging the living room, starting a new habit. The list could go on with the numerous ways in which we go through internal, intuitive processes that help us to organise and manifest. To do these things involves skills of time management, sequencing, budgeting, communicating, decision making, leadership, delegation, organisation, being proactive, and making commitments. With arranging your living room you would have considered aesthetics, energy flows, relationships between objects, interactions of people and many more factors.

We could consider this 'black box' designing, where it is happening without realisation of the steps we are taking. What you are about to discover is a way to make it a 'clear box' process; the Design Web will support you to see those steps and become more conscious and effective.

Our inner designer

We each have an inner designer, that part of us that engages with planning and organising. But most of us don't have a direct relationship with them; they are involved but not acknowledged, valued or specifically trained. Through using the Design Web regularly we will grow our inner designer. Growing in confidence, in visibility, in ability, in experience, in flexible thinking. They grow through feeding off all the myriad of transferable skills and life experience that we realise that we can bring into our work. Each of us has a unique talented inner designer. They grow through reflection on our process and learning about how we operate. They grow through embodying the spirit of adventure and learning how to interact with the Design Web. As we deepen our understanding we will see different facets of our inner designer getting exercised. As with getting fit, little and often is more effective than one big workout. It is through regularity and going through the process several times that we learn quickly and become competent. As your relationship with your inner designer develops, you will learn to trust their wisdom and they will flourish and grow in confidence, skills and competence.

From the small to the big

Imagine yourself using design every day. When you are planning a trip away, when you are organising the week ahead, learning a new skill, changing jobs; leaning into design to RESPOND TO LIFE. Imagine seeing the world through a designer's eyes. Imagine it becoming your operating system. You see solutions, possibilities, options. You see **patterns** that were previously hidden below the surface, you see **limits** and ways to jump over them. The small actions of your life become imbued with the purpose of your bigger **vision**.

Now let's expand our imagination and imagine that there are millions of people all around the world also in touch with their inner designer; people being proactive in their lives and communities, believing they have the chance to make a difference. Millions of people that are speaking the same language of the Design Web and activating their inner designers to turn their life into adventures. We collectively have the motivation and tools to tackle the big problems of pollution, poverty, climate chaos, sexual violence, and habitat destruction. At the heart is the goal of growing the ethics of Earth care, people care and fair shares. Design is part of the solution for humanity to co-create a world in which everyone's needs are met, where every person, being and ecosystem thrives and lives in harmony.

> "*Designing is an unfolding journey, it gets deeper, and wider and clearer with every step, even though there might be some foggy times along the way. I have the sense that when each one of us tunes in, finds and lives by what we feel most naturally drawn to, we will all organise harmoniously.*
>
> Ana Mouga, Portugal

> "*Designing implies awareness and from awareness of what can be improved, it is a small step to imagination and manifestation. If many more people would take conscious steps into designed responsibility for their own life, the world would be a much better place!*
>
> Barbara Scheltus, Croatia/the Netherlands

> "*Being a design adventurer is about finding balance, connecting with nature and living the life I want to live in a complicated world. My vision is for more and more people to discover design and feel more alive and in love in their lives.*
>
> Anna Gurney, Spain

Respond to life

Introduction to permaculture

Permaculture is many different things and each person develops their own relationship to it. Some might say there are as many explanations of permaculture as there are people practising it. Permaculture can be thought of as a movement, a community of practice, a design system, an ethical approach, a way of thinking and seeing the world. Some people are more focused on their own projects, others on community building, others on using it for cultural and policy change.

A lot of the definitions commonly used are outward looking and focus on what we do and produce, or tools and techniques and outcomes. I prefer to think of permaculture as something that starts within and ripples outwards. Whilst you could be mistaken for thinking permaculture is just about gardening, it has much to offer everyone, regardless of whether you have access to land or not, and can influence every corner of your life.

It started in the 1970s in Australia when Bill Mollison and David Holmgren first coined the term. They were heavily influenced by indigenous world views and practices, particularly local Aboriginal practices of relating to and caring for the land. The word 'permaculture' is a contraction of permanent agriculture. Permanent in this context means something that can continue to last and doesn't degrade or erode. This is based on the fact that indigenous people have tended land for millennia without degradation and that modern cultures need to find ways to do the same before we destroy the ecosystems that we depend upon. Over the decades permaculture has expanded and evolved to have more focus on people care and now it is known as 'permanent culture' as well.

At the heart of permaculture are three ethics: Earth care, people care and fair shares. These ethics are where we are aiming for. The path and enjoying the journey are as important as the destination, as it is an ongoing process. We live in an imperfect world which does not prioritise these ethics, so we also won't be able to fully inhabit them. We need to embody and live the ethics as best as we can, while moving towards them.

On the journey we use principles and design to guide us. The techniques and tools we use are chosen strategically. The principles were originally based on indigenous wisdom and observation of nature, and how natural systems are cyclical, productive and healthy. These same principles are adapted to make productive and healthy gardens, communities and lifestyles. These principles are brought together in strategic and thoughtful designs to create the solutions we need.

Before action comes design, which begins with observing land and people. Our ideas are tested out on paper to find creative solutions. We are both designing for nature and with nature. Through permaculture we discover purpose, community, hope, and different ways of seeing and interacting with the world. It encourages internal shifts that then radiate out into our lives, interactions, relationships, work and gardens.

My journey with permaculture

Permaculture has been a part of my life since 1999 and I have been a permaculture teacher since 2003. On the first course I attended, the renowned Permaculture Design Course (PDC), I was as much inspired by *how* I was taught, as by what I was taught. It was fun, engaging and participatory. My mainstream education had been very much based in traditional paradigms of hierarchy, where learning is top down. On the PDC we were all invited to share solutions, co-create and have fun. The beginner's mind was welcomed and listened to. I was inspired to stay involved by the people I met; the way in which we were all invited to be part of the solution and contribute to the movement right from the start. Through permaculture I have found my life mission and friends to journey with. I have been able to develop and share my gifts and skills. I can't imagine my life without permaculture woven through it. I'm very grateful for all that it has given me and so many others.

Back in the early 2000s permaculture was still focused on land. From my own experience and in conversations with others I knew that it had a much wider impact in people's lives than just how we garden. Permaculture has a habit of permeating our thinking, this then ripples out into all our work, activities and relationships. I wanted to share this magic with many more people, and I know that not everyone has interest or access to land-based permaculture.

One of my teachers said to me once that we already have all the solutions for widespread Earth care and repair. The question then becomes 'why aren't we implementing them?' The answer to this is invariably about people, whether that is managing our own time and energy levels, to dynamics in our relationships, the cohesion of our neighbourhoods, the policies and priorities of our country, and all the way up to international politics. In permaculture when we identify a limit, it becomes a need, something that we focus our attention on. So if people are the limit then increasing our people care skills becomes the need.

These strands led me to writing *People & Permaculture* in 2012, which is the first book to translate the principles and directly focus them on the people care ethic. From this time there has been a lot of momentum towards embracing the need to focus on people care within permaculture. There is now a growing body of work with various names – social, inner, people, personal, community – permaculture.

The methods and movement continue to evolve and grow. There are also many offshoots, where people take it into a new specialism; this can have its own name and particular focus and characteristic.

My own journey with permaculture continues to weave with others while expanding the knowledge of people care.

Introduction to Cultural Emergence

Cultural Emergence is an example of an evolution of permaculture. It has grown into an international movement of change makers.

Cultural Emergence came into the world in 2016 when Ruth Cory connected Jon Young with me. She had a vision of mutually beneficial exchange, with my work with the Design Web being useful for Jon, and his work with deep nature connection, and his 8 Shields model enhancing my work. We agreed to collaborate on a course together. There was evidently a big overlap between our work. On this course, however, instead of each teaching our familiar topics, we chose to actively seek what was beyond this, and move into unknown territory. We sought to bring things together to create something new. And we named this new entity Cultural Emergence. A fresh chapter began.

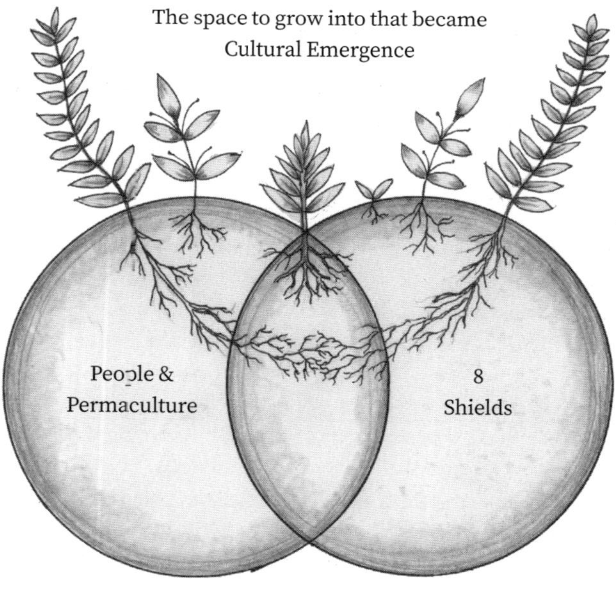

The word *emergence* actually arrived first, I had named this as one of the underlying qualities for my pathway design for the year and it seemed appropriate to use it for this collaboration. We felt that there was something unknown, mysterious even, that would arise. Then we realised that culture was a focus in both of our work. Jon has spent his life exploring the questions of why some cultures are more nature connected than others, and how we repair cultures, so that they serve to connect us. My work has been focused on what is needed to make the cultural shifts that reprioritise Earth care, people care and fair shares. How do we bring about these changes on individual and collective levels? The first line of a poem arrived – 'This cultural emergency calls for a Cultural Emergence'. The framing of Cultural Emergence thus came into place.

We realised that the ecological, social, political and personal problems that we face currently and in the future are a result of cultural problems. It therefore follows that attending to cultures to turn them into healthy, nourishing cultures will enable healthy, nourishing solutions to arise.

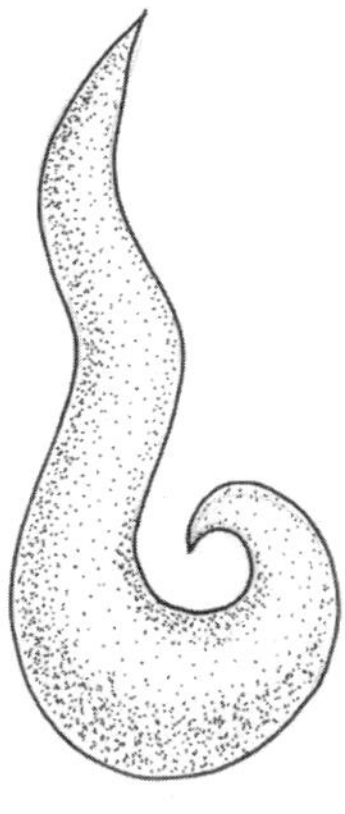

My symbol for emergence

Emergence is the phenomena present throughout life where new things arise in combination with other things. The fusion of hydrogen and oxygen gives us water; the addition of heat with selected ingredients gives rise to a cake; when a seed is buried within the dark soil, exposed to warmth and moisture, it cracks open and grows. Each of these examples shows that the characteristics of the new entity are not present in the original ingredients. There are new emergent properties.

When we bring culture and emergence together, we share the possibility of emergent properties that could arise in our cultures that enable us to shift into a regenerative future. The quantum leap that is needed for humanity to thrive and care for the planet could be possible through cultural shifts.

We both deeply hold a vision, which so many millions of people share. The Cultural Emergence vision is to **accelerate global cultural transformation towards a peaceful connected world to bring people and planet into alignment for a positive regenerative future.**

Visions of the future may seem very far away, and we need to find a way to bring them closer to reality. A mission is what you focus your attention on and where and how you choose to be proactive, in order to bring your vision closer to reality.

Our mission became **to create a profoundly effective toolkit to challenge and awaken, move and invigorate, nourish and empower individuals and communities.**

We involved other thought leaders in the process of creating the toolkit, in particular co-facilitating courses with Maddy Harland, Starhawk, Andy Goldring and Peter Cow. Over the coming years, through many processes of harvesting collective wisdom and careful thought and conversations, the toolkit evolved with premises, phases, practices, principles and pathways. We will be exploring those in the context of designing throughout this book. (You will see them highlighted in the text in SMALL CAPS.)

MANIFESTING THROUGH DESIGN AND ACTION is the keystone practice of the MOVE AND INVIGORATE phase, that this book is focused on. Although the Design Web was created before Cultural Emergence, it has been shaped and grown with the rest of the toolkit. There have been new layers of meaning and application that have come from the interaction of all of the tools.

Since my book *Cultural Emergence* and the CEED (Cultural Emergence Empowerment & Design) card deck have been published there have been thousands of people globally engaging with the toolkit. Our mission of creating the toolkit has been successful. Our second mission is now to encourage and empower networks and communities of practice to use the Cultural Emergence toolkit. Cultural Emergence is a growing global movement of change makers. As you embark on your own adventures, you become part of this collective emergence that is co-creating solutions and moving us towards a regenerative future.

Origin story of Design Web

Writing *People & Permaculture* was an ambitious endeavour to explicitly translate permaculture principles into people based systems; to bust the myth that permaculture is just about land and to make permaculture relevant to everyone. I did this while I had two young children at home and I accomplished it by using the tools I was writing about to support me. If I was writing about self-care, I was actively incorporating it into my daily life. When I was focused on the being effective chapter, I imbued the wisdom into my own being.

At the beginning I did a design for my process and how to overcome the limits and challenges of not having much thinking space within the family home. I created ways to be nomadic and used a basket I had made myself as my writing basket. It is practical and also symbolic of my ability to create. We cut a hole in the wall of the very small garden shed for some light and threw an electric cable down, and put a little desk in there, and voila, I had a writing shed that was so tiny there were no distractions for me.

It was in this shed that the Design Web appeared. I was focusing on how to describe the design frameworks used in land permaculture for people. I thought that it would be fun to create a more poetic acronym than some of the traditional permaculture frameworks. While I was thinking of different words to describe the stages, and hence different letters, I was also pondering which order things come in. Does vision precede ideas, or vice versa? What is the relationship between the making of decisions and creating an action plan? Surely you can't do one without consulting the other? With these questions in mind, my pen started to draw out a web of connections, and I realised the non-linear nature. The Design Web took its first breath in the world.

Over the coming months I spent many hours exploring, refining, and playing with the Design Web. I watched spiders weaving their webs for inspiration. I put cards on the floor for each anchor point and danced between them, feeling the essence of each one in my body, sensing the connections and flows between them.

I used the Web itself to create the Design Web. Well that's quite a meta level of looking at things! I would ask myself: What are the **patterns** to bring in here? I would go for walks in nature and I would focus on the **vision** for this new framework, imagining all the people that it could support.

I used the Design Web again and again to support my writing of *People & Permaculture,* my life, and my family at this time. These were our first adventures and they felt empowering and trailblazing. I have continued to use it in my everyday life. Since then thousands of people have also used it in their own lives and experimented and designed all sorts of things that I couldn't have predicted. There has been a weaving of collective experience that continues to grow our collective wisdom.

Step into the unknown

Overview of the Design Web

The Design Web is versatile, holistic, flexible and intuitive. It is a way of making the invisible visible. The Design Web has twelve 'anchor points'. They are highlighted in bold in the text. These anchor points each hold part of the information and inspiration needed for the design. The anchor points are grouped into four phases which show the development and how this resonates with natural patterns of growth.

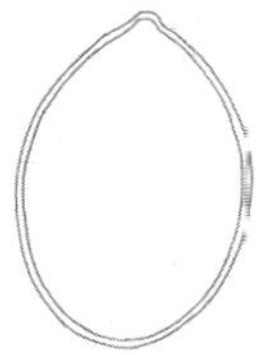

The *growth* phase – **vision, helps** and **limits** – is represented by the seed illustrating the potential of the vision, and what is needed to help it grow. It is congruent with the child phase of life.

The *exploratory* phase – **patterns, ideas** and **principles** – is the young adult or apprentice stage of life of learning, searching, and reaching out. The seedling is growing both its shoots and roots.

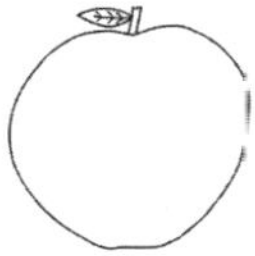

The *productive* phase – **integration, action** and **momentum** – is the grown-up stage of life where we are focused on being effective. The apple represents the yields that we get from our design through our activities.

The *reflective* phase – **appreciation, reflection** and **pause** – is archetypal of the elder. The mature oak tree illustrates how this phase grounds the whole design.

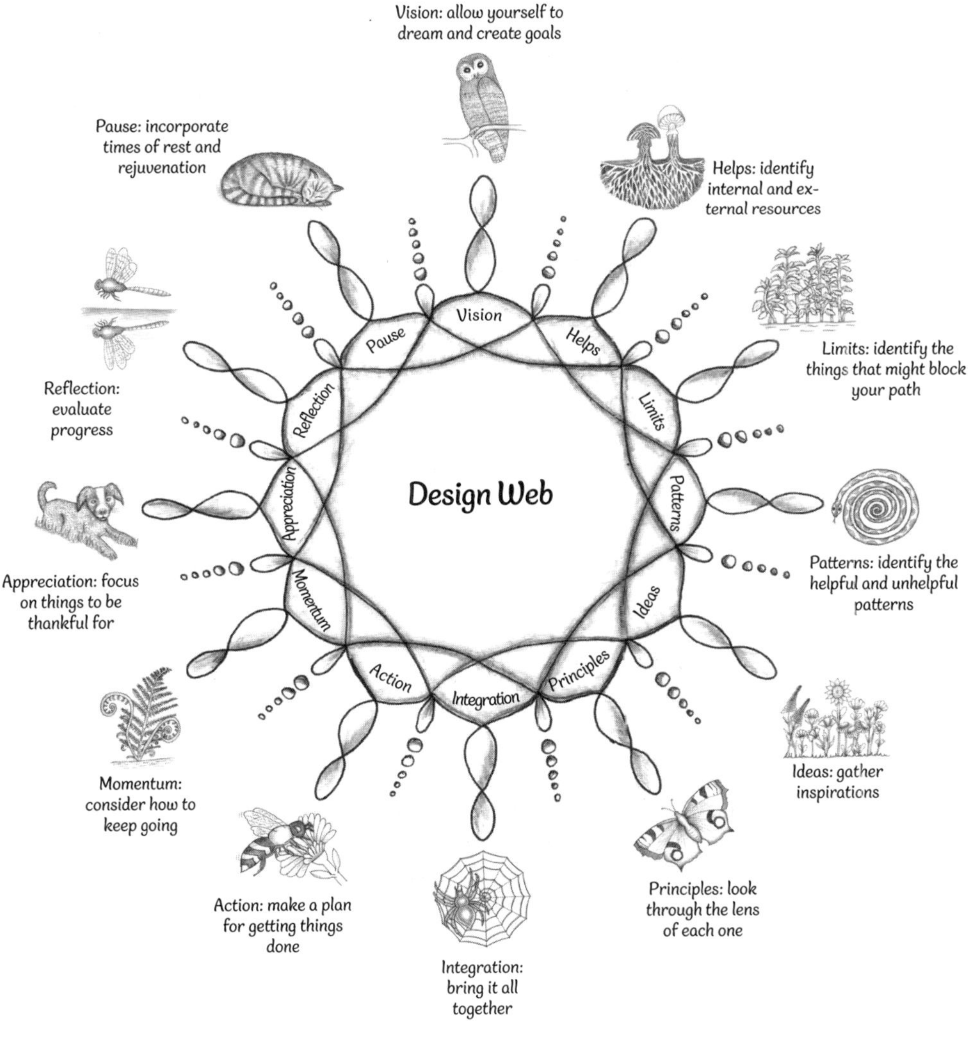
Vision: allow yourself to dream and create goals
Helps: identify internal and external resources
Limits: identify the things that might block your path
Patterns: identify the helpful and unhelpful patterns
Ideas: gather inspirations
Principles: look through the lens of each one
Integration: bring it all together
Action: make a plan for getting things done
Momentum: consider how to keep going
Appreciation: focus on things to be thankful for
Reflection: evaluate progress
Pause: incorporate times of rest and rejuvenation
Design Web
Vision
Helps
Limits
Patterns
Ideas
Principles
Integration
Action
Momentum
Appreciation
Reflection
Pause

The Design Web is a non-linear framework and you can weave between the anchor points in any order. Whatever the sequence there will be a flow of ideas, reflections, observations and questions and insights. Some tools, questions and answers respond to multiple anchor points simultaneously. Bringing the threads of thinking from each anchor point to the surface means we go from a tangled ball of wool and weave them into a beautiful tapestry of support. These flows and connections arise spontaneously or can be consciously created recognising weaving patterns, like an experienced weaver.

Essence of each anchor point

Vision

What would you like to happen?
What are the abundances you want to create in your life?
What are your wildest dreams?
Allow yourself to dream and create goals

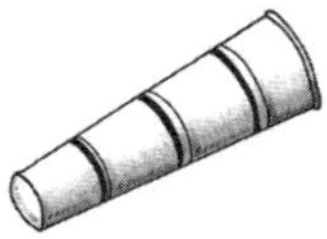

The symbol for **vision** is the telescope showing how we look into the distant future. Vision is our North star at the top of the Design Web.

Helps

What support and skills are within and around you?
What are your motivations for change?
How can you be helpful?
Identify internal and external resources

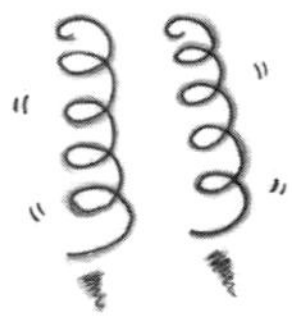

Imagine **helps** as springs on your feet propelling you forwards towards your **vision**. Helps show us all the many resources that can support growth.

Limits

What is holding you back?
What are the hidden, invisible limits?
What are your hesitancies and self-limiting beliefs?
Flip, reframe, view or use limits differently

The block shows all the **limits** and things that could block our path. Awareness of the many things that may stop us or slow us down helps us to navigate ways around them.

Patterns

What are the helpful patterns in your life, design, group?
What are the unhelpful patterns to transform?
What patterns can you bring in?
Look at nature's patterns for support

For **patterns** we have the spiral illustrating one of nature's many patterns, it is also repeated within our own bodies. It is a pattern of growth.

Ideas

What creative, adventurous, wild and wacky ideas can you imagine?
What big, little, practical, routine ideas do you have?
Who can you ask for ideas?
Gather abundant inspirations from many sources

Having **ideas** is like having lightbulb moments. Invite aha moments, flashes of inspiration, seeds of ideas, glimpses of solutions.

Principles

What principles support emergence?
What principles are present for you now?
What ideas do principles give you about the direction you want to take and how to get there?

The symbol for **principles** is the magnifying glass. Look through the lens of principles for guidance.

Integration

How can you integrate all the information gathered from the rest of your design?
What are the needs of your design?
How can you meet those needs?
Bring your design together and make decisions

For **integration** we have the web. Integration is the place where you are weaving your thinking together.

Action

What are you going to do and when?
What steps do you need to take now, soon and later?
What yields and benefits will your actions bring?
Make realistic budgets of time, energy, people, money

The bee represents the movement of **action.** Bees are constantly productively working. Be strategic and effective.

Momentum

What do you need to do daily, weekly, seasonally for maintenance?
What support might you need to keep moving towards your vision?
What slows you down?
Build momentum as your project, confidence and effectiveness grow

The swing for **momentum** illustrates the steady rhythm that builds over time, embedding the design into our lives.

Appreciation

What can you appreciate about other people and the world around you?
What are you grateful to yourself for?
How are you and your design supported?
Build in regular moments of appreciation

The heart shows **appreciation**, bringing us into a space of connection. It invites an expansive gratitude for all the support we have.

Reflection

What is the current situation?
What's been challenging?
What's going well and what yields and benefits have you gained?
Reflect regularly on your progress

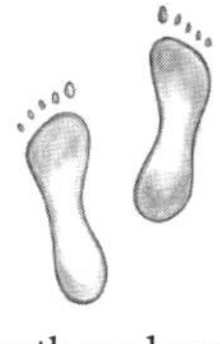

Footsteps show the path we have walked in **reflection**. **Reflection** invites us to observe, review and learn.

Pause

How can you build self-care into your daily life?
How can you revitalise your relationships?
How can you weave in rest, fun and creativity?
Incorporate times for rest and rejuvenation

The hammock is a wonderful place to **pause** and relax.
People care is woven throughout with nourishment and empowerment.

Guide to activating your inner designer

The first opportunity you have is for a quick design for how you can engage and interact with this book, and activate your inner designer. You might feel like it is a distraction and you want to just keep reading with a thought that you will maybe come back later, but just 20 minutes now is a worthwhile investment. This will support you in tuning into what you want to get out of the book, and identifying **patterns** and **limits**. It is a design that you immediately implement, and you can return to if you get distracted or need more **momentum** on your journey. Not only will it support your engagement with the book, but it will immediately familiarise you with the Design Web.

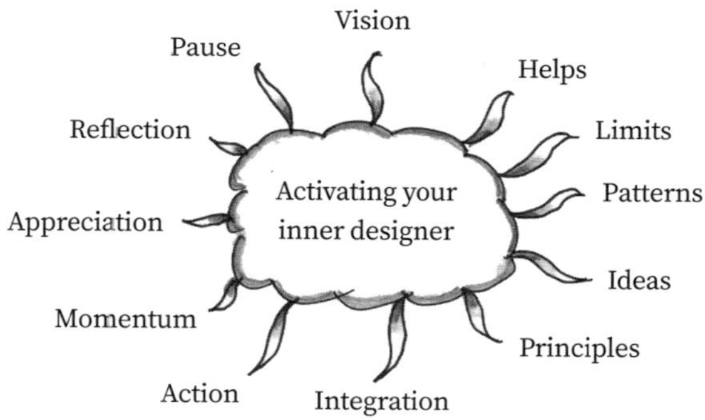

Set yourself a timer for 20 minutes (you can add more time after if you wish). Grab a piece of paper or notebook and some pens and get started. In the middle of the paper draw a circle with each of the 12 anchor points around the edge. Add your responses and answers to each anchor point below. Some of the questions are to answer now. Other anchor points give you things to do while reading.

Allow it to flow without overthinking or second guessing your answers, just write down the first things that come to you. If you can't think of anything for a particular anchor point then just move on and come back to it later. As you continue reading, add to this design, or go back to it if you lose momentum with reading.

This book isn't just about reading it from cover to cover, it is about engaging with it and doing your own designs. There is an accelerated learning principle, 'learning comes from active creation, rather than passive storage of information'. You learn best by doing what you are learning about. With each design you do you will learn more, and understand more layers and create your own relationship with the Design Web and your inner designer.

Questions and activities

Vision – Connect with the feeling you would like when you have befriended your inner designer and increased your skills through reading this book. Write down three words or a phrase.

Helps – What is your motivation for becoming an adventurer? What are the skills and qualities you have gained from other learning journeys? (This could be any skill you have learnt, or something small like trying a new recipe.)

Limits – What are the things that might distract you from reading and designing?

Patterns – What are the patterns of reading that work for you? What are the patterns that don't work for you?

Ideas – What ideas do you have for designs?

Principles – Look at the principles list on pages 182-186 and choose one principle to support you. Write or draw this and put it on your wall somewhere noticeable.

Integration – Which of these needs is a priority for you? Increasing design skills, designing with others, making changes in your own life, learning Design Web, building confidence.

What needs do you have that will support you designing? Creating space to design, scheduling design time.

Which of the ethics do you want to grow in your life – Earth care, people care and fair shares?

How do you avoid the distractions that you identified in limits?

Action – What's one achievable step you can take this week on your path? Gather supplies (notebook, large paper, coloured pencils etc.). Tidy your desk or create a space to do your designing.

Momentum – Feel your design muscles grow. Start with simple ones and increase confidence as you go. Is there a time of day or week that you could create patterns of reading and designing?

Reflection – What are your key learnings and insights from what you have read so far? At the end of each reading session, and at the end of each part, take time to write down your key learnings.

Appreciation – Take a moment each time you pick up and put down this book to appreciate yourself for taking time.

Pause – Where, when and how can you read and design in ways that are nourishing for you? For example, being outside, or in front of a fire, or in the bath or in bed. Would you like to talk to friends about it?

Reflection on the process – How did it feel to begin your first design? What did you observe about your inner designer?

Now that we have begun our design adventure we are ready to continue, from designing our week to whole ecosystems of interconnected designs.

Part 2

From microgreens to ecosystems

Use emergence to support emergence

There are different scales of complexity, depth and scope. A common mistake is for people to launch in at the deep end and try and design their entire lives. Carpentry tools have the ability to build houses, but as a beginner we would start with a bird box. Designing has the capacity to transform lives, projects and communities, but first we need to learn the skills. Use these scales, from microgreens to ecosystems, as guides to help you find one that matches your current availability and supports your growth.

Design possibilities

All around us are a multitude of possibilities. Processes, places, products, projects and pathways can be designed. For each role in our lives there are many layers we could attend to. Our parenting for example could have endless options from choosing schools to morning and bedtimes routines to family mealtimes to self-care as a parent. For ourselves we can focus on aspects of our health and well being, our effectiveness, learning new skills, organising our wardrobe. With others we can find collaborators, map communication flows, build community, start projects.

Microgreen designs

Microgreens are leafy vegetables that are deliberately grown to be small and harvested young, it is a very quick cycle of only a few weeks from sowing the seed to harvesting. They are vibrant, full of life and packed with nutrients in their beginning stages of life.

A microgreen design is, as you would expect, very small. A little pocket of your life. A single step towards where you want to be. A small improvement, a little adjustment and streamlining. I call them microgreens because we quickly get a nutrient-dense harvest. We benefit from the nutrients that feed our confidence and our inner designer. Even in their simplicity they can have profound impact.

One of the keys to success is to have a clear boundary. Designing our week ahead is a classic example of one. There is a definite ending to it. We are able to do the thinking, implement it, complete it and reflect. By doing the entire cycle we are able to really learn the tools. Time, space, and location are all ways of creating boundaries. Time is the most defined and the easiest way to keep it from expanding, and we know when it is complete.

Some ideas for microgreen designs:

- Today
- Stopping something for a day e.g. no chocolate, a day off social media
- Starting something for a day e.g. yoga, guitar practice
- Shifting our mood right now
- A meeting
- Preparing for something
- Getting one small area organised
- Tidying and cleaning a cupboard
- A celebration meal
- Giving a presentation
- Job interview
- Staycation
- Trip away
- A group gardening session

The idea is to go for what's right in front of you, something that is present for you in this moment. Choose easy and joyful things, especially when learning the Design Web. You want your first adventures to inspire many more to come.

Designs have a habit of expanding as we see the interconnections between different patterns and parts of our lives. When this happens, to avoid this overexpansion, roll things over into the future. Just observe what else wants to be taken further, and have a page in your notebook titled 'ideas for future designs'. It may only be the start of the story, the first chapter. Expect it to lead on to more designs, questions, explorations and change.

Is there a way you can make it even smaller? How about just the morning, or just a corner of a room? Other ways of containing it is by making it a quick process. Work on one piece of paper, or just write three words, or set a timer for two minutes on each anchor point. Limit the number of needs you are prioritising and give them good attention. A microgreen design is intended to be a quick nutritious snack, not to grow a whole garden.

When you have had the adventure, take time to reflect upon how the experience was different. Was there a shift in your feelings and attitude? Did anything happen that was unexpected as a result of the design? Soak in the benefits and nutrients and direct them towards your inner designer. Identify the harvests and share your story with someone.

Designing your week ahead

One of the first things I recommend you doing is designing your week ahead. This could be shortened to your weekend or even a day. You can decide whether your week is a working week, or seven days, or maybe a longer time is appropriate for you. The important thing is that there is a time boundary that is achievable for you to focus on.

The time boundary ensures that you have completion. You get to see the whole cycle of looking ahead, doing your week and knowing when that is complete and being able to reflect upon your week and your process.

Adventures are often open ended, leading on to the next thing and not knowing what the next chapter will bring. While this can be exciting in life, when we are starting out, it is useful to be able to complete and reflect before beginning another one.

The idea is to do this pretty quickly. Set yourself a timer for 30-60 minutes; this will depend on how long you have and the speed you like to work, or you can set yourself three minutes per anchor point. Get a large piece of paper (A3 or thereabouts or stick two smaller pages together) and with each anchor point, write down three words for the questions given below. There are no right or wrong answers here, just what is relevant to you. You can make your paper as colourful and artistic as you like.

It might seem as if it is just another way to create a 'to-do' list, but there is a shift from what we need to do, to how we want to be. As your week unfolds, use the **reflection** anchor point to review how it is unfolding.

One of the main aims of this is to enable you to learn the language of the Design Web. To build confidence for you to step into more adventures. The best way to learn is from actually designing, and then immediately implementing it. Your week will happen anyway so your design is unavoidable. There are some reflections on the process questions given, which will help you extract learnings and patterns, rather than focusing on the details.

Designing your week adventure guide

Reflection Start with reflecting on your usual week or the week just passed.
Roses – what went well, what was beautiful?
Thorns – what was challenging?
Seeds – what are the lessons to take forward?

Vision What are three qualities you would like to have?
How could the ethics be present in your week?

Helps What are three internal skills you have to support you?
What are three external resources you have around you to support you?

Limits What are three things that might stop you, or block your path?

Patterns What helpful patterns do you have that you want to encourage and enhance?
What unhelpful pattern do you want to reduce or let go of?

Ideas What ideas do you have that would help you with your vision?
Go for quantity of ideas; you don't need to do them all. Having lots of ideas will open up your creativity and feeling of possibilities.

Principles Pick two principles to support you from pages 182-186.

Integration Look back at your thinking so far and pull out the needs. Here are some ideas and you might have others as well.

- organisation
- tidying
- cleaning
- planning
- writing
- learning
- marketing
- nature connection
- connection to other people
- self-care
- family care
- rest
- creativity
- positive self-talk
- creating space

Some of these needs are around 'work', some 'play'. But you might have other ways of categorising your needs. Choose three or four most important needs for the week ahead.

Defining our priority needs is a valuable step. "The most important thing is to keep the most important thing, the most important thing." Jim Kwik

Revisit **ideas** for ways to meet those needs.

Action Here you can either choose to create a structured schedule for yourself for the week, or you might like to just think about three next achievable steps and when you are going to do them.

Momentum What are the simple daily practices that you can do or are already doing that will bring momentum?

Appreciation What do you appreciate about your week ahead?
When, how, and with whom, are you going to bring in some rituals of appreciation?

Pause How can you build in some rest, fun, play and creativity to rejuvenate yourself?

Reflection When will you take some time to reflect upon your design? For example, do you want to take 10 minutes at the end of each day, or half way through? Think about your own natural rhythms and what is manageable for you.
At that time ask yourself – am I on track? What is emerging?
Stay observant during the week. How are you responding to challenges? Make a note of these as you go.

Reflection at the end of the week What happened differently because of doing the design? (Of course there can be no control to know what would have happened without it.)
Did you feel differently about your week?
Did you have any unexpected yields?

Reflection on the process Answer these questions at the end of your designing and again at the end of the week.
What did you notice about how the anchor points connected?
What will you do the same or differently in the future? For another week ahead? Or for something else?
What did you discover about your inner designer?

From planning to purpose – Susan Cabezas, Chile/Ireland

Introducing the Design Web into my life was incredibly inspiring. I've always enjoyed planning and writing to-do lists, but many of these ideas never materialised. I used to label myself as a planner, not a doer, which limited me for years. The Design Web challenged this mindset and helped me adopt a new approach to organising my life.

For the past year, I struggled with low energy, lack of motivation, and a sense of purposelessness. I felt stuck – no clear direction, just ideas spinning in circles. The Design Web offered a way to move from endless planning to actually manifesting my ideas. It made me more aware of the process, allowing results to emerge naturally rather than through forced effort.

I first did a microgreen design for one week, and the results were transformative. I followed through with my plans and enjoyed the process, something I hadn't done before. Since then, I've consistently used this approach for more than 16 weeks, and it has become a key part of my routine, boosting my energy and sense of accomplishment.

Changing the focus: from tasks to a wider vision

My to-do lists used to focus on individual tasks, which often led to lost motivation midweek. I didn't have a clear sense of purpose behind the tasks. With the Design Web, I now start with **vision**: What do I want to happen this week? What resources are **helps** for me, and what **limits** and obstacles might block my progress? Answering these questions shifts my focus from isolated, sometimes even boring, tasks to a broader purpose.

Once I define the vision, I create **action** steps that support it. These actions no longer dominate my week but are part of a larger system that nurtures my well being. I also make room for **pause**, **reflection**, and moments of **appreciation** and celebration, which invigorate me and makes my weekly designs a healthy pattern to maintain.

From planning to purpose: the transformation

The Design Web has transformed how I approach personal growth and productivity. It has aligned my daily activities with a broader vision, bringing new enthusiasm to everything I do. This method has also deepened my awareness of my **limits** and resistances to change, helping me find creative, steady solutions. The image of a snail often comes to mind – a reminder that meaningful change happens through patience and thoughtful action. Fresh inspirations have come after this journey, including Design Web workshops in Spanish, creating a planner journal following the web, a model for workshops, and many more.

Seedling designs

Seedling designs are the next step up from microgreens. Not huge ones but a bit bigger. Seedlings have the potential to grow bigger, but for now we are germinating the seed and getting something growing. The seedling may look remarkably different from the seed of an idea that we have. When we start a seedling design we may not be aware of whether the seedling will grow into a huge oak tree design, or a quick growing salad. Bringing it into a seedling design gives us a chance to see what the plant will look like if we give it more attention. It is a chance to go from nothing to something.

At times we may need to repeat ones of the same thing to support incremental growth. In the garden if we sow lettuces all at once we end up with a glut that we don't know what to do with, followed by none. Succession planting allows us to have a steady harvest. We might do repeated or similar ones for aspects of our home or self-care or meetings.

Examples of seedling projects are a morning practice, gathering art supplies, creating a space to make, transitioning from one place to another, or one season to another, spring cleaning, family mealtimes, bedtime routine, getting children to school on time, reorganising your desk/garage/kitchen, digital organising, less caffeine, staying hydrated, regular artwork, cutting down on an unhealthy habit, work experience, healthy eating plans.

The seedling design may be a prototype for future ones, that then get expanded and repeated, such as a rainwater harvesting system in one area. Designing a lesson plan that then forms a template that is replicated in similar ways during a course. They are a chance to try something out that we might like to develop further, such as taking a week off eating sugar.

You could focus on the beginning stages of a project, how to bring people together. We may all need a design to find time to do our designing! Seedling designs expand our skills and influence.

Fruit designs

Fruit designs are when we are intentionally aiming for something to harvest. There is a visible and tangible product at the end. This could be anything from a book to a course to an art project. There is a boundary, a destination we are heading for. This may or may not have a specific time for harvesting.

Any event could be a fruit design, such as a course, birthday party, job interview, funeral, wedding, baby shower. As are creative projects such as painting, knitting a jumper, making a promotional leaflet, an exhibition, a calendar. Decorating a room, buying something, translating a book, making signs for your site, getting a pet, all have a specific outcome that you are heading towards. Changing jobs and moving homes would be large fruits.

Fruit designs are very satisfying, with something real and juicy manifested.

Root designs

Next we have root designs. These extend our support systems. Like roots they are mostly below the surface, but without them a tree cannot grow. The more extensive our roots, the more we grow, the more we are able to contribute to the world. Root topics include our health, effectiveness, relationship dynamics, and group culture. Ask yourself what roots are needed to support your ability to grow and fruit? They are focused on inner growth that leads to outer growth.

Root designs could be focused on one of our invisible **limits** that we have identified elsewhere, such as lack of confidence becoming the topic of building confidence. A few years ago I realised that there was a limit that was repeating in many of my designs. I had repetitive sprain injury (RSI) in my right arm and that was affecting every area of my life. I decided it was time to find ways to resolve it, or at least minimise it as best as I could. I named it Regenerative Arm Movement (RAM) as I wanted to call in what I wanted, rather than repeat what I wanted to get rid of. Doing this gave me strategies to solve the problem, and to keep my awareness open for when it is on the horizon and have ways to intervene and prevent it. By doing this I then increased my capacity and effectiveness in all areas of my life.

Root designs could be: getting fit, creating organisational systems, decision-making processes, nature connection journey, strengthening our back, social media presence, reframing self limiting beliefs, overcoming addictions.

Rites of passage and transitions could be either root or fruit, depending on how specific or spacious they are, such as growing into elder hood, regenerative parting from a relationship, leaving home or menopause.

Root designs, with other people in a relationship, group or workplace, are incredibly valuable in providing stability and security. The Design Web helps us to see in the dark. With root designs we travel into the underworld of our consciousness and see the hidden personal and collective patterns. It enables us to weed out unwanted habits and water healthy ones. By attending to your group culture, there is a sense of safety. Naming the culture we want frames our intentions, such as cultures of care, effectiveness, shared leadership, connection, confidence, trust.

We can't always see the results, but we can tell that it is improving the overall health of the system. Root designs are open-ended adventures that continually draw up nutrients. There is a flow from here into all aspects of your being. The deeper your roots, the more able you are to weather any incoming storms.

Design ecosystems

After a while you will have many designs: one design invariably branches into many, one adventure inspires another. One of the ways in which we avoid them expanding into something so all encompassing that it becomes unwieldy and overwhelming is by chunking it into smaller, bitesize ones.

We might want to zoom out and see the bigger picture, or we might want to zoom in and focus on a particular detail. Both approaches have their benefits and challenges. Zooming out allows us to see more of the interconnections and flows. Zooming in gives us the chance to reveal layers and depth.

With a land based project you can choose topics according to area or by theme, such as the water, compost or firewood, which may be in multiple locations and move through the landscape. Taking this into your own life, choose ones that are based in one area, or choose a theme, such as your creativity, or organising your paperwork. They then connect up to create an ecosystem.

Another way is by defining a time boundary, such as this year's spring cleaning, which would connect with the autumn clean and ongoing cleaning designs. Some designs become nested within others. You might have one for overall self-care, and then have other self-care ones for specific circumstances, like when you are travelling, or facilitating a course. These more specific ones are ready for you to step into when you are in these situations.

For big projects there might be different phases, each with its own needs and challenges, that need specific attention. When starting out we might need to overcome procrastination and lack of confidence. In the middle stages navigating frustration and boredom could be the focus. And then a design for all that the final stages of completion bring, such as fatigue and pressure.

For the CEED deck I did several designs; it started with visioning and a design called Playful Engagement, then I did one for regular artwork, another one for my Kickstarter campaign, and then one for BEAUTY IN COMPLETION. After a while I realised that I had missed a design for promoting and selling it; this became Seeding the CEED deck. At each stage the new design brought fresh energy and momentum. The whole project is nested within the bigger plan for Cultural Emergence called Going Global. Translating the CEED deck into multiple languages is another one that addresses the **limit** of it only being in English and widens accessibility.

An event, festival, business, organisation, farm, or project will have many interconnected designs. Building a home would need multiple ones. A course programme could have many repeated similar designs.

Within your own life you will have many diverse projects, some hugely interwoven, some with only very distant, barely visible connections. When designing one part of our life over here, it connects to a thread in our life elsewhere, that we might not even have been aware of before we started. But suddenly it becomes apparent that there is another area awaiting our attention. They also connect with the threads of other people's life adventures.

Multiple designs are not usually a linear journey from one to another. They become lots of moving parts in our lives, each with their own timings of activity and rest. Some will have times of hibernation, while others are growing fast. They interact and there is interplay and give and take between them, the **limits** of one design might spark **ideas** in another design. **Helps** in one become the **momentum** for another. Each supports growth in others. Making progress in one design may then enable us to revisit a previous one and go deeper and further. Designs nudge each other, growing alongside one another. Some decision making happens across multiple ones. A design for working at home would connect with a design with housemates for keeping the house clean, and another for plentiful pause and community connection. Experienced growers will successfully grow many crops in one season, whereas beginners are better off just focusing on a small amount. You don't want to spread yourself too thin; it is worth considering how many you want to start at any time.

Decision dominoes – Delvin Solkinson, Canada

The Design Web has guided me on an adventure into a new chapter of life. Reading the book *People & Permaculture* unlocked something deep inside me, a belief that something meaningful and magical lay ahead if I only had the courage to leave the comfort of my current life and be open to the emergence of something new.

Setting out from my tiny coastal rainforest village in British Columbia, I knew I needed to travel to Applewood Permaculture Centre to learn in person with Looby but I had no idea where this would lead. The course transformed my life in the best of ways, aligning me with a deeper sense of direction and purpose, giving me more courage, confidence and competence. When I first start I assemble 12 different pages, writing the title of each anchor point on the top of each page and adding art and photographs that represent each anchor point visually. Next I visit, and revisit each page in relation to my topic: a garden, an introduction to permaculture course, a deck of permaculture cards, and my work at a non-profit arts organisation. Soon the pages are filled with notes. Choosing which ideas and actions I would actually do from the brainstorm, I write it up in a shorter form, highlighting things that are implemented. With each opportunity to practice, the Design Web became easier to use and increasingly effective in supporting me to make decisions.

In order to share with groups, I have made large pieces of paper with each of the anchor points on them as words and pictures, then laminated them for outdoor use. Placing the anchor points in appropriate locations, like **momentum** half way down a hill, and **limits** on a rocky outcropping, the journey becomes a physical adventure of walking around a garden, farm or forest location outdoors. Pairs of people rotate around the different anchor points in an interactive and collaborative journey, supporting each other to bring more intention into something practical they are about to do in their life. Working as part of a community of practice has brought me together with many fantastic people, giving me inspiration to dream big and take action to achieve my dreams.

A breakthrough moment in my journey was understanding that it can enable new possibilities to emerge in many different areas of life. Using the Design Web to focus on a specific project often yielded support, momentum and yields in other, related or even unrelated parts of my life. I have also come to realise that designing can be a fun and collaborative game as well as a way to find guidance and direction.

In the past 10 years I have used the Design Web for the whole ecosystem of my life. As a toolkit, compass and springboard for my decision-making processes, it has supported me to move to a different country, change careers, get married, focus on my health, facilitate courses, complete a Permaculture Diploma, and even to co-create a collaborative Group Diploma program with Looby. Each new topic emerged from all the work I had already done, a domino of designing that was increasingly propelled by its own momentum.

Leading me through a process of discovery, the Design Web is helping me transform the mundane into the meaningful and magical, unlocking new opportunities, relationships and projects.

Design metaphors

Don't worry if you aren't sure whether it is a microgreen, seedling, fruit or root design. You may start out thinking you are doing one type and then realise that actually your root design could be contained and be a microgreen design, or your seedling one is ready to fruit. It doesn't really matter, these are just ways in which I've found it useful to share the scale of the different possibilities.

The important thing is that the scale matches your current need, attention and capacity. If you choose one that is too big for what you are able to do now, in terms of confidence, time and commitment, then it can become a burden rather than a help. Equally too small may not give you the fullness, detail or momentum that you need right now. What is the level of detail that is useful for you right now?

There might be other metaphors that feel good to you. Maybe your design feels like something else – a red kite soaring on the thermals, a warming fire, a mole burrowing underground, a cat about to pounce, a flower bed for pollinators, a feast for friends, a sailing boat. A hummingbird design is fast and fluttering, an oak tree design is slow growing with immense strength. There are so many ways to describe your adventures.

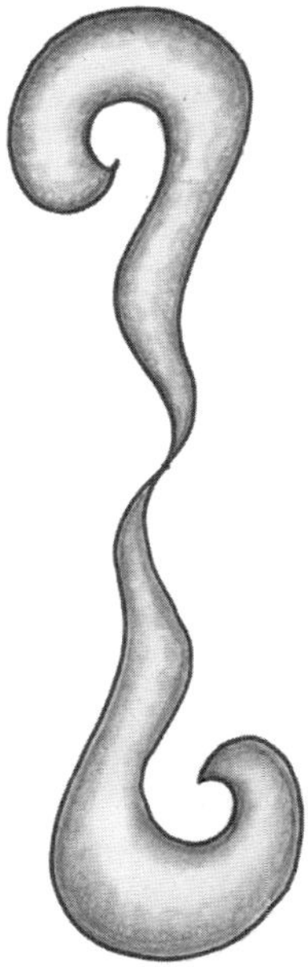

Use emergence to support emergence

Receive encouragement

Choosing another design

There is a time when you realise how many possibilities there are around you. Every plan, every interaction, everything that you've ever wanted to do, every corner of every room in the house could benefit from some design input. And it can be overwhelming. Where do you start? There is a tendency to either spread yourself too thin and start multiple ones simultaneously but not get further than the beginning stages. Or to be paralysed by choice and not do any of them.

Essentially there are two approaches: one is to bring your designing to where your life is right now, to improve, streamline and support, and the other is to go where you want your life to be, to grow, evolve and adapt.

A good starting point is choosing which scale you want to do: microgreens, seedling, fruit or root.

Map out the options that you see around you. Then ask yourself the following questions, circling ones that apply. Afterwards you will see the ones that have the most circles and choose from these options.

Ask yourself:

- What is planned in your life already?
- What is unlikely to happen without a design to give you momentum and commitment?
- What are you going to most appreciate having done?
- Where's the sparkle?
- Where's the energy?
- What needs help, support and energy?
- What's right in front of you?
- What do you need to move forward?
- What's present for you right now?
- What do you want to streamline, fix, enhance, invigorate?
- What do you want to grow?

For beginners, I suggest you choose ones that fall into the microgreens category. When it's something that is going to happen anyway, it will ensure that it is completed. You will be able to streamline the event and learn the tools. By choosing something you are already familiar with, you will give yourself a chance to become familiar with the Design Web rather than dealing with two unknowns at once. Recognise where you already are and build on your existing skills and confidence. Stretch but don't overstretch.

As you develop your design muscles you can do ones where there is no energy but energy is needed; a simple example would be turning a hate of the washing up into loving it. Even something so seemingly simple will have layers and nuances within it. But to start with, keep it really simple and manageable.

Starting with yourself is the place of most influence and will enable you to observe the effects more clearly than when co-creating with others.

Doing a design can sometimes feel like we are adding another spinning plate, when we are barely able to cope with what we are already doing. Instead, turn this around, and think of it as a tray that will help you carry all the plates that you are holding in your life.

Threshold of commitment

At some point you will feel yourself crossing a threshold of commitment. It is a feeling in your body of enthusiasm and motivation, a sense of 'can do, will do'. A confidence and surety of that is going to happen one way or another. It is the equivalent of going from looking at travel guides to having bought your ticket.

This threshold can happen at different places. Sometimes it happens as soon as you have chosen to do it. Other times it is further along in the process. Often the naming is a significant point on the journey. Sometimes it is more of a subtle growing of commitment, and you perhaps don't realise that you have stepped over the threshold until afterwards, perhaps when talking with a friend.

Sometimes after a while you realise that you don't want to do it at all, and something else emerges that is more captivating. This is OK and part of knowing ourselves and is a valid outcome.

Often just reaching this threshold of commitment is in itself of huge significance.

Naming your design

There is a potent time when we give it a name. This naming gives it form and direction. Choosing a name that describes what we are trying to bring in means that we are continually repeating this. The name can be poetic, resonating with the essence of what we are visioning. It may be more down to earth, and a 'say what it is on the tin' approach.

I discovered the significance of naming when my partner Chris and I were trying to manifest some land as a home and venue to hold courses. After many years of wishing for it we decided to cross the threshold of commitment with a design. We spent a long weekend weaving our way through the anchor points. We named it Land Search. It included a **vision** of what we wanted to do there, which we wrote up to show to other people. Only a few months later we were offered a beautiful piece of land to buy. We fell in love with this land and were delighted to go ahead. We planned to move closer while we applied for planning permission to build a home. This didn't happen though; every house we looked at we got a 'no' in one way or another, with houses suddenly being taken off the market and random reasons happening. After over a year of this we realised that we needed to go back to our plans. Although we had found land, it didn't feel complete, we hadn't included our home in the name! We realised that **limits** had changed, new limits were there, which we hadn't expected around finding a home nearby, and also some of our previous limits around being close to schools had changed, and we could widen our location options. It was a difficult decision to give up this land and look for somewhere else. After making that decision we renamed our design Finding Applewood.

A few weeks later after looking at many places we arrived at our dream location. It was an immediate YES the first time we came here. We are lucky enough to have Applewood Permaculture Centre as our home and course venue, inviting people from all over the world to come and learn with us and from the beautiful land and beings here.

From then on, I have been very careful with naming. I really try to make sure I don't leave out anything important. Around this time a friend was feeling her biological clock ticking and wanted a baby. I reminded her not just to focus on the baby, but to include a loving relationship as well. Happily she found the love of her life, got married and had twins within a year and a half.

Take some time finding a name. It is helpful to do this at the early stages, but don't worry if it doesn't come right away. Sometimes I find the name easily, other times I need to do some thinking before the name arrives. You will be repeating the name often so make sure you are repeating what you want to call in, not what you want to let go. Reducing stress repeats the word stress, whereas increasing calm focuses our attention on the word calm. What is the problem you are trying to fix? Then how can you name the solution and put the focus there with the name; giving up smoking could become healthy lungs.

Find something that is memorable and motivating. Names often get shortened so either make it short to start with, two or three words works well, or make sure the shortened form works as well. Weave together both action and feeling into the name. The name is a poetic portal into possibility.

Design names

Here are some names from course participants and diploma apprentices, that you could read as a co-created poem.

Starting strong
Moving forwards
Nurturing emergence
Activating flow
Spiralling upwards

A village seed
Growing wings
Growing a village
Growing together
Nourishing vibrant roots
Nourishing souls
Facilitating resonance
Embodied resilience
Enabling ease

Embracing a way that works
Regenerative work
Activating the field
Sharing stewardship
Transformation in community
Inclusive inner designer
Collaborating with a diverse global team
Balanced people care
Making sense

Step it up
Genius peace and ease
Going global
Becoming mentor
Celebration of service

Leading from the heart
Building baselines
Energising cycles

Seeds of change
Seeding future
Wilderness network
Inviting the wild
Tree joy
Wild living
Reclaiming our indigenous nature

Garden gatherings
A shrine for design
Beautifying for effectiveness
A home for my creativity
Space to make
Clear way
Sacred time, my magic
Finding my voice
Cultivating enoughness
Being my own best friend
Reclaiming my heart song

Celebrate to manifest
Beautiful movement
Vision to action
Flying free
Coming home
Emerging into greatness

Design Web as friend and mentor

Doing microgreens regularly means that we become more and more comfortable and competent. This regular flexing of our design muscles increases our agility in problem solving. Over time the Design Web becomes part of our operating system, part of how we see, feel and function in the world. The Web becomes like a helpful friend to rely on. Like our friendships, sometimes we have a quick chat, other times long in-depth conversations, and occasionally a full weekend visit. It acts as a mentor for us, in an age when many of us don't have elders and mentors in our lives; the Design Web is available to us at any time for support and listening and advice. In the same way that we might have imagined conversations in our head with an absent loved one, we can turn internally to its wisdom and have an internal dialogue. It is there on your shoulder cheering you on, showing your blindspots, keeping you on track and inviting you to invest in your dreams.

Receive encouragement

Trust the process

For each design there are stages we go through from the preliminary stages, then the active thinking and exploration and then implementing it, and then reflecting. In the preliminary stages we are making the decision to start, then defining our focus, gathering resources and setting up systems, whether that is digital or with paper and pens. If designing with others we are setting the culture and establishing guidelines about how it is going to work. We might set ourselves a timeline. In the active stage we will be writing notes, compiling observations, having ideas, making decisions, plans and commitments, and fitting the jigsaw together. Implementation will involve trying things out and making changes and carrying out the action plan. The principle BE ATTENTIVE TO SHIFTS, OPENINGS AND OPPORTUNITIES illustrates how you can follow options that resonate with your needs and vision, and adapt and flow with changing contexts. The implementation leads you to the next version – the next season or chapter, or more detail or other connected designs. These stages might overlap each other.

Starting points

As I've said, the Design Web is non-linear and you can jump around the anchor points in any order. This also includes starting at any one. There can be impetus for starting with any of them. The seed of an **idea** or a strong **vision** might encourage you to find ways to manifest it. It could be a **reflection** process that makes you think, 'let's do it better next time'. You might lose **momentum** and want to regain it. Your project might hit **limits**, or there could be a crisis or emergency that you need to navigate, a problem with a capital P. It might be some negative **patterns** that you want to break free of. A time of **pause** such as a holiday could be used as a turning point. **Integration** could be the anchor point that you jump straight into with a need to be met, or a new system coming in. Any of these things could provide the initial push and also indicate where to start.

Some might be centred around one or two anchor points with the other anchor points explored in relationship to these. A design for effectiveness, for example, is mainly about **action** and **momentum**. You would then be looking at your **patterns** and **limits** etc. in connection to **action** and **momentum**. Self-care designs are focused around **pause**. Creating a **vision** could be the aim in itself.

Twelve page download

A good way to start is what I call the 12-page download, or 12-page blurt. It is a way of quickly getting your thoughts out of your head and onto paper. As you might expect, it involves getting 12 pages of paper, or 12 pages in your notebook.

With a microgreen design, one large piece of paper is sufficient and helps to contain the thinking. Moving on to bigger ones, some more space for writing is helpful. In between the one page and the 12 page options, is to use four pages, one for each of the four phases with three anchor points on each page.

In the middle of each page write one of the anchor points, and if you have your name already then add that in as well, such as Harmonious Home **Vision**, Harmonious Home **Limits**, etc. I prefer to use unlined paper and to have my paper in landscape rather than portrait, but find your own way. Add colour, pictures and doodles as you wish, to brighten it up.

Now you are free to jump around and add thoughts as they come. You might want to work on each page for a specified time, or you might want to just jump around intuitively. It's really up to you.

What people often find is that they are already aware of many of the answers, but they were all jumbled up in their heads. Doing the 12-page download allows all of it to come out and we can start to organise our thoughts. When we are either unsure of where to write something or see the same thing occurring in multiple places, it illustrates the connections between the anchor points.

After doing this we can reflect on the process, which ones came easily and which were more challenging? Which anchor points gave you the most insights? Are there similar patterns with other designs?

The 12-page download is there ready and waiting for us to add insights as we continue about our lives. Sometimes most of our thinking can be done in this way and it is enough to lead us to action and change. Other times it is just the starting point and we can continue with bringing in more tools, such as deeper questioning, artwork, nature connection and body wisdom.

Ethics

The ethics of permaculture are Earth care, people care and fair shares. There are many different ways of describing the third ethic of fair shares. The original term described by Bill Mollison was 'limits to population and consumption and reinvest surplus'. This was shortened to the less wordy fair shares. Other terms used are future care, parity, living within limits, sharing surplus, mutuality. In essence all the terms are about sharing with other people, future generations and other beings. All three of the ethics overlap with each other. They are about finding ways to live in harmony with planet and people.

All of our designs need to be contributing to these ethics in some way. It might be a small, personal increase in our people care, our relationship to Earth, some small way we are sharing. If the ethics are not at the centre then we cannot call it a permaculture design. It is a fundamental outcome to grow the ethics. Of course we would like to live in a world that fully embeds all three ethics, but currently we are not there, and it is not a final destination or quantity of ethics that we want to achieve, just more than we had before. If we are moving away from the ethics rather than moving towards them we are going in the wrong direction! It cannot be permaculture if we are planning for something outside of the three ethics, such as a war, or a nuclear power station.

I am often asked why there is no ethics anchor point. I see the ethics as embedded into the whole process; they can be visited in any anchor point. Think of the ethics as three wise elders, ready to offer their advice whenever we approach them. They are overseeing the whole process, urging us to come closer to them. They give us unique insights in relation to different anchor points.

Pause and **appreciation** are explicitly increasing our people care, and we can also widen our appreciation to include Earth care and gratitude for all the more-than-human world. (I use the term more-than-human rather than nature, as we are also part of nature.) Our motivations for each ethic could become part of the **helps**. Within **limits** we can think about the limits to how much we can take. With limits we can also ask – how is it hard to meet the ethics? What's stopping them from being present in my life? How do I limit my consumption?

For **integration**, growing each of the ethics could be a specific need identified – and then systems to increase them. Looking at the ethics in **vision** is a way of bringing them alive in their highest possibilities. **Principles** could become the principles and ethics anchor point.

Revisiting the ethics often throughout will give you greater understanding of them and you will begin to see your designs as a service to humanity and part of a bigger vision.

Traps, challenges and solutions

There are many ways that things don't go according to plan. Some are delightful surprises, other times though we get stuck in the process or confused. Accept this as part of the process and something to work around.

One of the challenges is that the problem can seem larger than before we started. When we bring it to awareness we see the layers and complexity of the issue, whereas before it was under the surface or only just in our peripheral vision. We might wish to take it out of our view again, and give up. Knowing this is part of the process helps us to stay with it.

Another challenge that appears in various ways is the distinction between designing and doing. While some are about designing and then doing, often there is an intermingling of both. It is not one and then the other, there is an overlap. However, this can lead to either thinking, 'I've started doing now, so there is no point in any more designing' or in contrast, 'I can't do anything until I've finished designing'. Both of these are traps that restrict our progress. Of course we are able to start doing things before finishing all our thinking, often in fact there is an initial burst of energy and enthusiasm when we decide to focus our attention. If we are doing a spring cleaning project, there is a layer of obvious work to do, that we can get on with, while we also determine how to get the deeper work done. After this initial input though we still need to discover ways of going deeper and maintaining it. When organising an event we can set dates and announce them before we take time to work out a detailed timetable.

As we become more experienced, design thinking happens spontaneously while we are doing. The danger then becomes that we think that we don't need to do the designs themselves, and that it is all happening in our minds, so it is unnecessary to put it on paper. This is another trap to be aware of. The goal of meditation is that life becomes a walking, living meditation; this is only achieved and maintained through a regular meditation practice. The goal of designing is that design thinking becomes an automatic way of seeing the world; this is achieved and maintained through doing regular, thoughtful designs on paper.

Another challenge is having too many, or that one has led on to another, and the first design is abandoned. This can roll on and on, with none of them ever being completed. This is where doing microgreen designs is so useful. We get to see the whole cycle and learn a lot in the completion stages.

Either focusing on too much detail, or taking too big a picture can lead to confusion, overwhelm or missing important connections. At any point you might want to change your boundaries and switch from detail to big picture or vice versa. Another pitfall is that quick designs stay on the back of an envelope, never taken forward and developed more, or written up. Or they are done and then put away and forgotten about and we go ahead and do something different, or fall into our old patterns. This is why later you will learn about creating something in **integration** that is representative of the whole design, that you leave in sight. Whenever you see it, or hear it or touch it, it is a portal into all of your thinking.

One of the reasons for getting stuck is that your brain tries to understand the solution and jump ahead, rather than letting the design itself do the talking.

Another tendency is to start with something simple like your week ahead and then go down the rabbit hole of childhood memories, cultural work ethics and patterns and before long you have attached the entire human history and evolution. To avoid this trap, keep asking yourself what is important and relevant to now and what could be for the future.

Unsticking

There are times when our designs get stuck somehow. This could be around any of the anchor points: finding our **limits** overwhelming, not being able to articulate our **vision**, having too many or too few **ideas**. It might be in the transition from design to **action**, and trying to make it real. It might be through lack of time, or too much pressure to 'get it right' or solve the problem quickly. Being stuck might be about forgetting about it and putting it to one side without the motivation to revisit it. The feelings of being stuck might show up as frustration, confusion, blame, anger, or guilt. Instead of a complaining mindset and blaming yourself, other people or the design, take this as an opportunity to really tune in and listen more deeply to the design.

The first thing is to accept where you are at, and to realise that it is part of the process and doesn't mean that you have to walk away completely.

Beyond acceptance, here are some suggestions of anchor points to (re)visit to unstick:

- **Limits** – what are your current limits? Have any limits changed?
- **Helps** – who can support you now?
- **Action** – what is a very tiny step you can take? Choose something you are both able and willing to do, that you commit to do, then do it. After doing it, celebrate it and the pattern of success you are starting. Then think of the next tiny step.
- **Appreciation** – what do you appreciate about your designing so far? What do you appreciate about your inner designer?

Even if you don't make as much progress as you might have hoped, don't label it a failure or mistake. There will be lessons to learn, something to harvest from what you have done. These times of frustration will still be yielding you insights about your inner designer. Try a different design, something smaller, something that is right in front of you.

Being stuck might be because something else is emerging that is more relevant, exciting, and important to design. Following your motivation and enthusiasm is a valid way of finding your path.

I am frequently asked 'What is a good design?' A good design is simply one that is helpful to you.

When is a design complete?

Designs are unfolding journeys revealing themselves to us in stages. There will always be more layers that we could include and dive deeper into. At some point though, this becomes less useful to us. Like when we are tidying and cleaning, we might know that a corner of the room or a drawer, still needs cleaning or organising, but if we go to do that we will run out of time and leave the room in more chaos. We sometimes need to postpone it and WORK TO COMPLETION on getting the room to a respectable level rather than going into deeper cleaning. The scale needs to be compatible with your time and energy inputs. Moving the goalposts is allowed – move them closer to where you can reach them.

Designs are complete when they have had the desired effect; it has moved from paper to reality. This could be a very defined outcome with the materialisation of a product, such as with a fruit design. Often though they do not end, and are ongoing processes. We are often working with living systems which grow and evolve, so there is never an exact end point, where it is finished, before it then changes and evolves again. Designs become moving and dynamic systems. Completions may feel like arbitrary moments in some ways, a flag in moving sand. One way around this is to think of different versions, chapters, parts or phases to complete.

They can be considered complete, when they *feel* complete to us. One of the many benefits of doing microgreen designs and other ones that have time boundaries or other boundaries, is that you will get familiar with the feeling of completion. Even for a garden that is still growing and changing, you can have a sense of completion.

Another way it feels complete is when it has its own momentum in your life, for example when you don't need to write on your job list to do some yoga as it is now just a natural part of your way of life. It becomes an integrated part of our being, part of your personal or group culture.

One of the steps of completion is bringing it into a cohesive whole that is readable by others.

Documenting and writing up

There are two reasons for documentation: for our own benefit and enhancing our own understanding and keeping it active for ourselves; and writing it so that it is readable for others. Both ourselves and readers are enriched and framing our writing up as a service to others is motivating.

Many people have blocks to writing up; it seems tedious to them after the initial flow of creativity and action to go back and document it. Or there is a wounding from our schooling about getting it right or wrong, or a rebellion against perceived deadlines and word counts. To counteract that, we need to find our own intrinsic motivation and see the benefits that come from doing the writing up. Recognising that writing up is a chance to use your creativity and that there are no set templates that you need to follow is liberating.

If we are not making any notes at all, then it is just going around in our heads. It restricts our thinking as we try to hold on to pieces of information. On paper we allow the design to do the talking; we become the listener. The invisible becomes visible, our blindspots, **limits** and hidden **patterns** are revealed. With other people, having it written up gives accountability and a reference for decisions and actions.

There is a value in designing in our heads; I do it all the time. I also write books in my head, paint murals, make clothes, even tidy the house, and these lay good foundations for actually doing it, but it is essential to follow through. The principle MOVE THE TOOLS reminds us of this vital part of the creative process.

There are many yields that come with writing up. Designing on paper is a chance to make both mistakes and discoveries. We get to test out placements, sequence

action plans, articulate **visions**. Instead of planting a tree and then realising that it is in the wrong place, we realise this on paper first, where we easily try out many options. As we type up each anchor point, we might notice that one or two have much less than the others and seek to go deeper. Discoveries come from noticing gaps in our thinking.

By sharing with others we are contributing to the body of knowledge, increasing the design library of Cultural Emergence. Other people are inspired to try for themselves, they learn from your process and have a head start on their own adventure. While each one is unique, people are able to read it and extract patterns and insights.

Writing up can be done as the design appears, so that you don't need to go back to this task later. This might involve a computer, or simply tidier handwriting. Documenting through photos is inspiring to track progress. Remember to take 'before' pictures and then photos from the same spot at regular intervals.

Another of the challenges is getting a non-linear process into a linear format. Some people like to go through each anchor point in turn, others like to show the process as it happened, revisiting some multiple times. Either approach works. There is a lot of useful online software these days to support creative presentations.

Including bullet points, flow diagrams, word clouds, maps and infographics makes the flow of text more digestible. The final design could appear as a blog, film, story, a series of social media posts, cartoon, drawings, photo essay, mind maps, slides, poem. We will come later to using artwork as a design tool, as well as bringing it into the design for visual interest and beauty.

In the online design library you will find many varied and creative examples of documentation. You may even wish to contribute your own to the growing library.

Reflections on the process

Nothing builds our design muscles and connects us with our inner designer as much as reflecting on the process. This is when we take a meta view at what we've done, how it worked, what we could have done differently and what lessons to take forward. We zoom out from the details and look at the patterns. We are learning from both our 'mistakes' and 'successes'.

Reflections on the process will help us learn about:

- ourselves as designers
- Design Web and tools
- particular types of designs.

Reflecting on the process is important for our own learning; the second part of it is its significance for the reader. For the reader this is one of the most interesting parts as it supports them to think about their own process. Through our reflections we are empowering the next generation.

Choose two or three questions from each section.

To learn about yourself

- How did I feel before and after deciding my topic?
- What skills have I practised?
- What do I want to do more of?
- What gave me courage?
- What gave me hope?
- What did I learn about my inner landscape?
- What skills do I want to practise in the future?
- What changed in me?
- What challenged me?
- What patterns in myself did I observe?
- What shifts am I going to make?

This reflection helps us to find our own strengths, as well as recognising the parts we find challenging, sticky, or boring. For our next adventure we will be able to lean more into the parts that excite us, and accept or reframe the other parts. And perhaps this time those parts will be easier. Plotting the process enables us to see the relationship between ease and insights. We might see the optimum length of our design sessions. These questions can be adapted when collaborating and everyone can share their reflections.

To reflect on the Design Web and tools:

- Which anchor points flowed easily?
- Which ones connected with others and how?
- Which tools did I use?
- How were they helpful?
- How could I use the tools with different topics? In similar or different ways?
- What other tools might have been useful?

Tapping into this reflective process can be done with more than just words. Drawing, movement, and nature connection are all tools we can use. We can bring in some numerical intelligence and plot our increase in skills and competence. Metaphor, storytelling and poetry can be used. We could describe our journey with nature's patterns, such as a wave or spiral, or draw a river to show the flows; what were the rocks and the waterfalls, what were the river banks holding it in place? Drawing a web of connections between the anchor points makes visible the interactions between them.

It is a chance to compare and contrast different tools, so that we make more informed choices next time.

For particular types

We are adding to the creative commons. Imagine a massive library of all the permaculture and Cultural Emergence designs that have ever been done; shelves upon shelves all grouped into different types. There are an abundance of shelves for gardens, and the knowledge for how to do these has been passed along, so designers have a good starting point. Other shelves for self-care designs are also full of many unique examples. Beneath the uniqueness of each one there are underlying themes and patterns. These will be mostly different for garden and self-care, but even here there will be some overlapping qualities, for example the importance of observation, the need for weeding and pruning. Understanding these themes and patterns will help us for other topics. It increases our fluency and confidence to try anything. Perhaps we feel inspired to try something where that shelf is almost empty.

Some ways in which others can learn quickly is by giving top tips for this type or the 'do's and don'ts'. What are the ingredients and the recipes for a particular topic?

Reflection on the process is done at many stages. Before we embark, a quick reflection on previous times is helpful. Continual reflections as we go means that we don't have to try and recall details from long ago. Small and often is better. Doing it frequently will harvest learnings as they happen. As soon as I start a design I have a page for reflections on the process, so that I harvest them as they occur to me. Indeed this book is only possible because of those continual reflections. Of course we can't see the full overview until the end, so that is a really important time to reflect.

One of the potential downsides of doing this reflection is that some of the magic might get lost. And through overanalysing and breaking things down into parts, we lose a sense of the whole. If you find this happening, then take a step back and try to take a big picture view, as well as using other senses. You will find the ways and times of reflecting on the process that work for you.

If we find ourselves getting stuck somehow, then reflecting on the process is a really valuable way of unsticking. Rather than attributing it to whatever we are designing, perhaps it is about the way we are approaching it. Are we putting too much pressure on ourselves to do it 'right'? Can we bring in more creativity? What happens when we take ourselves outside? Do we find it more useful to talk through things with a friend, or to have solo journalling time? Have we expanded too much and need to bring in the boundaries? Are we getting lost in the details? Our reflections will also help us to avoid getting stuck in the same way in future.

The reflections on the process will inspire us to take on more and more designs. Our competence grows and we become fluent designers. As with learning a language, we go from learning the basics, repeating standard phrases, to customising simple phrases, to being able to tell unique and complex stories.

There is such a rich strata of learning that can happen with the reflections on the process. The questions can be inspirational and juicy such as, what made you smile? What was magical? What surprised you about yourself? What was beautiful?

Golden keys

There are moments in your process where there is a sense of the pieces falling into place. When this moment occurs cannot be predicted, as it varies each time and with each person. But out of the chaos, confusion and indecision suddenly the path becomes clear. I refer to these moments as 'golden key moments'. There is suddenly an insight, idea, letting go, reframe or some other shift that has a cascading effect throughout. A reframe that means that now we see over and beyond our blindspots. A letting go that releases attachment and opens up a new opportunity. Imagine a Harry Potter door with cogs turning and golden sprinkles of magic flying about as the key turns. There is a cascade of insights. We don't know what's on the other side of the door but we sense its importance. The ripple of the golden key is felt throughout. When working with others it gives a new level of understanding and cohesion. Often the golden key appears as common sense and obvious, as if it was hidden in plain view.

The principle YOUR BODY KNOWS shows how it will immediately give you signals when you land upon a golden key; a sense of excitement, perhaps even nervousness as you anticipate shifts and stepping into the unknown.

While doing a design around regular artwork while creating the CEED deck, I realised that I was caught in a thinking trap of 'I can't do artwork in work time, because it's play, and I can't do artwork in play time because it's work!'. This realisation with the reframe of 'I can do artwork at any time' unblocked my **limits** and gave me a lot of **momentum**.

It is tempting to feel like your work is done after one of these realisation moments, but it is still valuable to ensure you have visited all of the anchor points, to reinforce the learning, and there may be still more golden keys to come.

These golden key moments can be beyond the design itself, and give us realisations about ourselves, or about the Design Web, or other designs, past, present or future.

Emergence

Through designing emergence happens. Emergence is when things come together to create something new. There are characteristics of the new thing that weren't present in the parts. These are called 'emergent properties'. Water has emergent properties that are not present in the gases of oxygen and hydrogen.

One thing leads to another and we get unexpected, surprising outcomes. Just as a plant looks completely different from the seed that was planted, our design can grow into something that is unrecognisable from our original intention.

Designing can take us to turning points in our lives. A friend started doing a microgreen design to create a space to do her design work. She found this more difficult than expected and realised that there were **limits** in her relationship that she had been ignoring, but were now surfacing. This led her to also question her job and whether to live in the city. Soon she had moved out, found the job of her dreams and left her partner. There was a cascade of interventions from questioning one thing that could have been simple, but highlighted other issues. She approached me saying, "Sorry I didn't keep up with the course", and I replied, "Please don't apologise, I think the design actually worked its magic, just not how you expected."

Sometimes the rabbit holes that we go down lead to rabbits, and other times we discover delightful treasures.

Quantum leaps in cultural shifts occur when our personal or group culture jumps to a new level of functioning. Our home culture of tidiness, for example, shifts to a new level of baseline functioning after we have deep cleaned and rearranged the furniture.

There is non-linear or discontinuous change involved in emergence. It often isn't a straight line of incremental changes. The proverbial straw that broke the camel's back refers to this. The final straw only breaks the back because of all the other straws before it, even though nothing was appearing to happen before. The straws reach a tipping point and then there is quick momentum towards the change. Tom Brown Jr talked of flocks of birds and how we never know who is the one bird that will turn the flock. It is always worth reaching one more person, as maybe they will be the person who turns the flock of humanity.

The principle USE EMERGENCE TO SUPPORT EMERGENCE shares how the emergent properties that arise allow for more emergence to happen. There is a snowball effect, although with emergent properties the snowball might morph into something entirely different along the way.

Synchronicities

Many people have observed the number of synchronicities that occur during a design adventure. People arrive with the right skills or messages. Morale boosters appear out of nowhere. Jon Young and I have often mused on this phenomenon as it happens so frequently to us. It feels like the universe is weaving threads together. As we start to play our parts in bigger stories of life, many other players come on the scene, and views open up. Our designs are part of someone else's life stories, we are opening up pathways for others to follow. As we come into flow, we come into alignment with natural cycles and rhythms and we experience more and more flow.

Belief in helping hearts – Jon Young, USA

Myself and many people have reported back an increase in synchronicity while using Design Web. You could also call it flow. For example, we might be overwhelmed at the scale of tidying a barn and then a friend will phone out of the blue, suggesting they visit and help out. I get to the point where I can't even count the synchronicities, it's unreal, and it feels like you're somehow tapping into the flow of the universe that helps not just in the design process, but then in the actual unfolding of the project. And then synchronicity goes off the charts. I wondered why and began to realise that Design Web has all the elements of sacred ritual. It's secular, it's not religious, it's not spiritual, it doesn't pretend to be. But there is a shared intention that creates a field that attracts this flow. The naming is almost like magic words. The intention is now bound up in the two- or three-word name. Every time you work with that name you're reasserting that intention, and you're charging up the system with this powerful intention.

I believe, because Design Web is coming from Looby's observations of the spider, and nested in the context of permaculture and the indigenous lineages that contributed to permaculture, there is a sense of purpose greater than self. We're not cleaning the barn for selfish reasons. We're cleaning the barn because we want to be able to create a space to give our neighbours and friends experiences that will help them live a better life, essentially. Oftentimes, when we're using Cultural Emergence, permaculture or nature connection principles in the **principles** anchor point, we're deliberately tying ourselves to be in service to helping the Earth be healthier for people and for all of life, we're trying to make a difference. We're trying to be conscious of how this benefits the Earth. How does it benefit all life forms? How does it benefit future generations?

I think those are all the conditions that are in a traditional indigenous culture. These things are all present in prayer and ritual, and they result in synchronicity. But here, there isn't the trappings of any particular spiritual path or religion. So it just invites people to go into even more humility, and they bring fun and joy into it, which also increases the energy of the field. These are the things that I've tracked that are contributing to the flurry of synchronicity.

I truly believe from experience that there is a lot of overlap between a vision quest and engaging with the Design Web. They have so many of the same sacred elements. Design Web creates space for emergence, which is exactly what you are doing on a vision quest. Design Web feels like a ceremony, but not tied to any religious beliefs, it's just tied to belief in creativity, belief in yourself, belief in helping hands, and helping hearts and minds of others. And challenging yourself to get out of those stuck places, and find solutions that transform the way you do things, and bring out your real gifts and your real power and effectiveness. Then the flow starts to happen. And this has been my experience every single time with Design Web.

Part 3

Weaving and dancing

The Design Web has 12 'anchor points'. When you look at a spider's web you will see that they find several fixed points to attach their web to, and then weave in between these. Each point anchors and supports the web. In the same way, each of these anchor points holds information and insights that support us as we weave the web between them. These 12 anchor points hold the design in place.

Each anchor point has a different kind of presence. They bring forth different qualities of our inner designer. Each one is capable of both releasing and giving energy. Releasing stress and confusion, giving us strength and hope. Through this pulse of release and gain, we are able to weave together an adventure that holds new possibilities. Each anchor point connects to other ones and we dance between them, weaving our thinking together as we go. It is the thread between the anchor points that creates the spider's web. There is an emergence that occurs through the inter action of all 12 anchor points, where a new whole with its own identity and strengths comes into being.

You could imagine each anchor point as different lands to visit on your adventure. Different tools and methods are used to explore each one. There are places to avoid and things to leave behind when we visit it. Each anchor point has a movement and way of embodying the essence. When I was creating the CEED deck, I looked to the more-than-human beings at Applewood for their archetypal wisdom relating to each anchor point. Different Cultural Emergence principles speak to each anchor point. There are cultural patterns relating to each one, and a liberation of our thinking and discovery of gifts as we engage with them.

VISION

Places to visit

With visioning we visit the future, it is a journey of our imagination and the more we fully embrace our creativity, the more full our vision becomes and the more excitement we generate. Having ideas is different from connecting with our vision. If we feel alive and energised in our body then we know we are on the right track and touching our vision. It is a chance to fully express our longings.

Bring your imagination and long-term thinking. Bring your ambitions and dreams. Allow yourself to use your imagination to turn your longings into visions that empower and motivate. Vision involves more than just our eyes; let your whole being be involved. How does the place of your vision feel, smell, touch, sound? Sense yourself in the completed design, imagine the joy, satisfaction and celebration. The more senses we bring in the more magnetic our vision becomes. Our vision is our north star guiding us.

Vision is about being of service to something greater than ourselves. It might just be a microgreen design that we are working on, but it is a drop in the ocean of positive change. Our designs are nested within a greater movement towards a better world. What wants to flow through us? What is growing in the design? How are the ethics growing? Vision is about us working collaboratively with the ethics to bring them alive, listening to Earth, listening to the needs of people, listening to our heart's desires. With vision we see ourselves as change makers. Ultimately vision is about asking the question 'how can I help to make the world a better place?'

The emergence of your vision comes with bringing longings, imagination and service together. Vision ignites hope.

Tools and methods for exploring

- Write an intention statement, starting with I intend to...
- Plant a seed while thinking about your intention. Write your intention on a label and stick it to the pot, so every time you water the seed you are watering your intention.
- Timeline – use some string or rope to lay out a path between now and a given future time. Walk the path up and down, stopping at imagined milestones to feel and celebrate progress.
- Backcasting – imagine a newspaper article from the positive future, what story does it tell of how we arrived there?
- Make a time capsule for your future self to open when you have reached your vision (this could be buried in the garden or in a sealed envelope in a drawer).
- Write a letter to or from the future.

- Goals and targets – put some numbers to your vision – how many people to reach, how many courses, numbers of books to sell etc.
- Time travel activity – imagine you are travelling to a place 5, 10 or 20 or even 200 years in the future, what is there?
- Write your vision and mission statements.
- Imagine your ideal scene, give it plenty of details.
- Guided visualisation
- Collective storytelling
- Create something to symbolise your vision – a collage, poem, photo, drawing, affirmation, movement, song, sound.

Wisdom from the more-than-human world

Widen your owl vision

Owls guide us through the vision anchor point. Owls are able to turn their heads almost 360 degrees. There is a nature connection activity called Owl Eyes. Expand your peripheral view by stretching your arms and wiggling your fingers in front of you, gradually move your hands apart while keeping your eyes facing forward, stop when your fingers are at the edge of where you can still see them. Owls use more than just their sight to find their prey, all their senses are engaged. Owls are often referred to as wise and insightful, and the collective noun is a parliament of owls. Owls' ability to see in the dark reminds us of looking beyond the surface, to see hidden wishes, patterns and dynamics. Owls remind us to embrace moments of stillness, dark and silence to find our vision.

Embodiment

The movement for vision is arms up in the air, stretched out, looking up into the sky or long distance horizon; bringing in the sense of possibility and change into our bodies. When the visionary spirit is activated within you, you feel excitement tingling, goosebumps, butterflies, a rush of energy.

When the visionary spirit of a group comes alive, there is a flood of inspiration, ideas and enthusiasm. The group feels connected and motivated.

Avoid

Leave behind your cynic and scepticism, they will just put a dampener on the party. Leave behind your realism filters. Think about what you would like to happen, not just what you think could happen. The principle ALLOW FOR THE POSSIBILITY OF THE SEEMINGLY IMPOSSIBLE reminds us to let go of these filters, and engage our visioning muscles beyond just what we think is currently possible.

Cultural awareness

There are cultural limits on the allowance of creating visions and being ambitious. We may have been silenced or ridiculed in the past for expressing our visions, small or large. If you are getting stuck then say out loud to yourself, and the whole group, if you are working with others – 'we have permission to dream big here'. You could write the word 'inner cynic' on a piece of paper and ritually place the paper outside the room.

Liberate and discover

Stepping into vision is recognising that things can be different. Vision connects us to our values and ethics. Our vision often calls for us to be bolder and braver than we feel comfortable with. As we feel in service to a bigger vision we find motivation to act. The principle BE IN COURAGE invites us to reframe nervous energy as courage surfacing. Our ambition and imagination dance together. When we speak our visions out loud, the universe listens.

Weave and dance

Vision – Ideas
Articulating your vision will give rise to ideas of how to bring it to life.

Vision – Limits
As soon as we express our wildest dreams and longings, we are likely to think of all the reasons why it can't come into reality. This takes us to limits.

Vision – Pause
In the stillness of pause we have capacity to dream into a greater sense of purpose and service.

Starting from imagination and dreams – Liz Postlethwaite, UK

For me, vision is our opportunity to push to the edge of inquiry and ask: What could be possible here? How would we like it to be? How might it be in our dreams? It is the anchor point that sows the seeds for something to emerge that is grounded in, and inspired by, the expansive and imaginative exploration of possibility.

Nature's Winter was a collaborative design creating a museum installation about climate, community and nature at a museum on the banks of Lake Windermere. Vision was explored through informal conversations and also through a visioning day. We used a range of creative activities to explore the idea of 'weather', which had emerged already as a theme to bind together multiple diverse threads within the final installation. We thought about what weather reveals, and what it can be used to investigate. We then went on to think about whose stories it may help us tell, and how these stories may be recorded. Finally we brought this all together to think about the gallery space we would be making the installation in and how we would like visitors to be able to interact and engage whilst they were in there.

It was through these activities that it became clear how important playfulness and accessibility were to the project. And also that the final installation should be ever changing, with community voice at its core, alongside a wider aspiration to engage visitors with the natural world. Here ideas that emerged in vision became the foundation to ground the way the project developed going forward.

On a different scale, within a design to structure a year of home education for my family, vision became a space to explore what was most important to us at that moment in time. We did this informally through conversation and more formally by sitting down together and mapping on paper what we would like to include in the coming months. We also looked back to reflections that we had recorded during the previous year to see what aspirations had been recorded there. Vision was a space where we deepened our understanding of what foundations would be key to our learning. The needs of core skills, development, new interests, balance and connection emerged and fed into **integration** and became way markers that we referred back to throughout the rest of the process.

Within both of these the foundations that emerged as a result of vision then became the central ideas that fed into **integration**. In travelling to the edges of possibility within vision it was possible to integrate in ways that felt both strong and dynamic at their core.

HELPS

Places to visit

With helps we are exploring, both internally and externally, resources that will support our adventure.

This is the time to really feel into our own resourcefulness and the amazing array of abilities we each have just to navigate daily life, let alone the specialist skills we have learnt along the way. Visit your cupboard of skills that you have accumulated, the organisational skills, self-care practices, people care experience, creative passions. While you might not know immediately how some of these skills relate, make a note of them anyway, their use might become apparent later on. At the very least they will be a boost to your confidence. Revisiting your life stories will illuminate the many times and ways that you have shown up and found ways to grow and contribute to make things happen.

Your motivation for change is a potent support for your adventure. Without this you are unlikely to make any significant change. Connecting with this motivation will propel you forward with tenacity and commitment.

Support comes from many different places, not just from ourselves. Other people are often the biggest source of helps, with their creativity, friendship, encouragement, and knowledge. Organisations and networks also provide connections and expert advice. The more-than-human world gifts us with grounding, energy, vitality, nurturing, wisdom, love.

Expand your awareness to the many different levels of helps. There are tangible, pragmatic helps, such as money, computer systems, phone apps, storage, filing systems, cleaning materials, lighting, bookshelves. There are also more intangible helps, such as time, values, and friendships. Creating even small pockets of time will be helpful.

Another dimension of this anchor point is to think of ourselves as being helpful – where and how and to whom can we be helpful? How can we be helpful in growing the ethics? How is your design being helpful out in the world? The essence of helps is reciprocity.

Helps is part of the growth phase, and brings visibility to the resources that are going to bring the vision to life.

Tools and methods for exploring

- Ask your friends and family what strengths they see in you
- Skills audit and mapping
- Make or revisit your CV

- Observation of your home – what objects and artefacts represent a skill or quality or time in your life?
- Reflect on something that you have done or made (this could be something small or something very significant). Think of the complex skill set that made that possible.
- Think of all the roles you have or had in your life. What are the skill sets for each role?
- Ask who, how and when can I help, hold, heal, nourish, empower, gift, lift up?
- Go into nature and ask, what is supporting and resourcing me now?

Wisdom from the more-than-human world

Be like mycelium and create symbiotic relationships

Mycelium represents helps. Mycelium is the web of fungi under the surface of the soil that connects plants and trees. Mycelium creates symbiotic relationships with plants, exchanging nutrients and information. Mycelium encourages us to look below the surface. Mycelium reminds us of the interconnectedness of life, it is a direct example of EMERGENCE HAPPENS IN RELATIONSHIP.

Embodiment

Imagine yourself with springs on your feet, effortlessly jumping along the path towards your **vision**, covering distance in leaps and bounds. Your time in the helps anchor point will leave you with a feeling of being resourced and a 'can do' attitude.

Avoid

It is easy to venture into the space of 'not enoughness' – I am not enough, I don't have enough skills, money, friends, colleagues, hours in the day and the list goes on, if we start on this route.

The other place to avoid is the complaining mindset. To start moaning about how we would have learnt this skill if only we went to a different school. Or that the policies don't support us. Or any number of other reasons.

Avoid being shy about yourself, underselling your abilities. Or thinking of yourself or others as arrogant for sharing your skills and amazingness.

Cultural awareness

We are deeply steeped in the 'not enough' culture. With each skill that we have identified we might also see that we would like more of it, to practise and develop it more. There is a sense of the more we know the more we realise we don't know. And the more we learn, the more we see that we have to learn. This can lead to us not valuing what we already have and know.

The lone wolf, 'I can do this alone', mindset is widespread and takes us away from linking up with others and benefiting from MANY MINDS ARE BETTER THAN ONE.

Liberate and discover

Helps is a journey of discovery. As well as seeing our skills, it reveals our gifts, our passions, our innate talents. Trust in our support systems can arise through listing all our external resources. It makes reaching our **vision** seem easier than we thought. This anchor point builds a lot of energy. Through helps we live the principle DISCOVER ABUNDANCE.

Weave and dance

Helps – Appreciation

Helps and appreciation are very compatible dancing partners, often hand in hand, in step with each other, intricately woven together. As we list our internal and external resources we appreciate them.

Helps – Limits

There is sometimes debate about whether to visit helps or limits after vision. Is it good to connect with our motivation and skills to move us towards our vision, and then have the reality check of limits? Or is it good to get the reality check of limits and then to boost our morale with helps? Either works and of course you can choose which order to do them in. There is a strong interaction between the two.

Helps – Momentum

Our resources are going to be important in giving us stamina and support to build momentum.

Cultivating abundance – Dharlyn Gomez, Philippines/Canada

Helps serve as a powerful reminder of the potential for growth and transformation when acknowledging and utilising the resources available to me. By reflecting on how I am transforming the areas identified in **limits**, I can make conscious decisions that align with my goals. I feel grateful for the universe's support and excited about the internal motivation that drives my creative efforts to manifest.

One of my designs is Seeds of Change: Cultivating Permaculture Awareness Across Cultures. During a two-month apprenticeship with the Agriculture and Technical Skills Development Authority Learning Center, managed by the CEP-AGCO Center for the Poor Agriculture Cooperative in Mindanao, Philippines, I became more proactive in harnessing my skills in project management and co-ordination as I became the volunteer coordinator. There were 30-90 volunteers at a time participating, from different senior high schools in the bioregion, during their two week immersion programmes as one of the requirements to graduate. This experience allowed me to engage in creative facilitation, sharing skillsets, tools, and wisdom through various hands-on landscape projects and activities.

The most transformative aspect of this experience was connecting with diverse cultures and demographics through deep listening. This engagement not only enriched my understanding but also highlighted the importance of empathy and collaboration in design. In helps I create a space for change by identifying my internal resources that significantly impact the design's success. I claim my potential and embrace a shift from scarcity mindset to an abundance mindset.

To support others in finding their helps, I role model being humble and open about my limits and needs as I implement projects. This creates space for people to step in and offer help and support. By sharing my journey, I encourage others to embrace vulnerability and seek support when necessary. This collective approach creates a nurturing environment where everyone can thrive.

I recognise that the external environment, including the ecosystems I belong to, the people around me, and the institutions and movements I engage with, are all resources that help meet my needs. This realisation leads to an understanding that I do not need to constantly yearn for more; everything I require is already available to me and will manifest at the right time. I am inherently enough.

Practising gratitude amplifies the positive impact of my actions, opening doors to new possibilities and opportunities in my life and the world around me. By cultivating a mindset of gratitude and appreciation for the interconnected web of support and resources that sustain me, I not only attract more abundance but also deepen my connections with others and the environment. This ripple effect of positivity inspires and uplifts those around me, fostering a culture of generosity, collaboration, and growth within the ecosystems I inhabit.

By embracing abundance and practicing gratitude, I have created meaningful designs that resonate across cultures and foster positive change.

LIMITS

Places to visit

Attention to limits is essential to provide a container. Without some limits, then yes anything is possible, but we don't have a channel for our energy. In a world where anything is possible how would we choose what to make possible?

Limits help us to pack the right resources to overcome future challenges on our adventure. This is the time to visit your honesty and courage.

There are visible tangible limits, such as policies, the shape of the land, the size of the room, the number of days of an event. Then there are invisible or under the surface limits, such as our beliefs, values, confidence. Both are influential and need attending to.

Some limits are to work within, others to overcome and others to reduce. Sometimes limits are absent and need to be brought in.

This is the anchor point to invite your inner sceptic back into the room and out to play. Give the devil's advocate a loud and prominent voice. HONOUR THE WISDOM WITHIN reminds us that they have some useful perspectives and warnings to share.

Visit the edges of your comfort zone, what's at the edge? We each have our own unique constellation of limits. What feels a stretch for someone and outside of their comfort zone is not at all limiting for someone else.

Tools and methods for exploring

- Observe your inner dialogue.
- Imagine an obstacle course – what are the obstacles?
- Reading your vision, start the sentences – Yes, but... or that will never happen because ... and see what follows.
- List all of your limits. Then use the principle YOUR BODY KNOWS to guide you. Tune into your body wisdom; what is your body reaction to each of the limits? Which limit gives the strongest reaction?
- Are there limits missing? What limits are needed?
- Flipping limits – turn your limits around into needs for **integration**. Your lacks become the things you are trying to grow.

Wisdom from the more-than-human world

Nettles are limits until we find a use for them

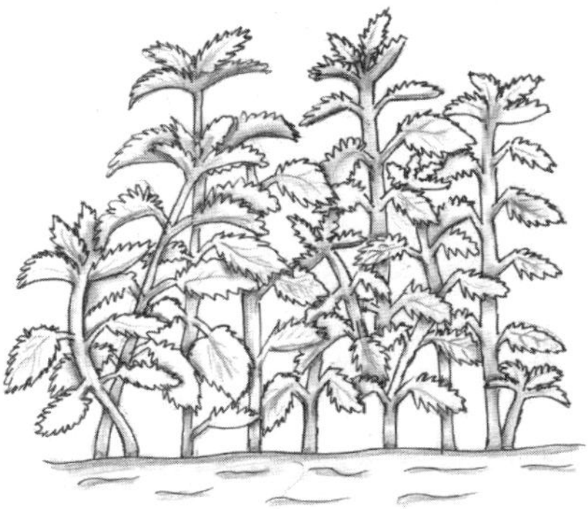

In a sense all of life could be a metaphor for limits; each being has created a life strategy that has adaptations to the limits of their environment. They work within the limits of their niche while also over time stretching their capacities, such as male deer balancing the biggest antlers to show virility whilst still being able to manage them on their head. Salmon swimming upstream is also a good metaphor for overcoming limits.

I have chosen nettles as they are abundant and widespread. Cut them back and they will regrow; we are never going to be short of them. They sting us, which is painful but it gets our blood circulating. They are a superfood and a plant with many uses, from fibre to liquid fertiliser to medicine. We just need to know how to use them and value them properly.

Embodiment

The initial focus on limits makes us feel small, perhaps curled up into a tight ball. Then with the flipping of limits into needs we feel ourselves unfurling. Limits moves us from overwhelm into curiosity and possibility. Our motivation is activated. There is a movement from contraction into expansion.

Avoid

Old limits may disappear but we don't notice and get trapped in an old story of 'can't'. Avoid getting caught in mental loops of perceiving limits and not noticing when they move, such as feeling the scarcity of space in the greenhouse, and forgetting the time when all the seedlings start moving out later in the season and the shelves start to empty. Or still living in the poverty mindset of student days when you now have a job and more financial security and don't need to buy the cheapest biscuits any more. Wider cultural limits, parameters and tolerances also change and release or create limits. The principle BE ATTENTIVE TO SHIFTS, OPENINGS AND OPPORTUNITIES is particularly applicable for shifts in limits.

Cultural awareness

Time and money will almost always appear as limits for most people with any topic. We have such strong and pervasive cultural conditioning about the lack of both, that these are the first things we think we don't have enough of. Our overemphasis on these can be misleading and be convenient excuses for not doing the things we want to do. We ignore other deeper issues, such as our limiting beliefs or lack of confidence. Cultural norms and expectations are key limits that we might ignore, take for granted, or think immovable.

Liberate and discover

Through identifying needs we have the opportunity to flip these limits into needs. They focus our attention on how to turn a lack into building it and generating more of it. For example, our lack of confidence becomes the need to build confidence. Our lack of money becomes finding funds as well as reducing financial leaks and costs. In this way limits are thought of as the building blocks of the design.

As well as paying attention to the more obvious limits, we also sense into the more subtle barriers. The limits anchor point gifts us the opportunity to speak the usually unspoken, to express our hesitancies and resistance. Through speaking them it allows them to shift or us to recognise what we don't want to, or can't shift.

Weave and dance

Limits – Principles
Living in connection with the principles does require us limiting some cultural norms and behaviours.

Limits – Helps
There is a strong relationship between limits and helps. Are we valuing what we have as a help or just in a scarcity mindset and seeing the lack of it as a limit? Viewing our limits can then lead us to valuing what we do have and also to finding more of these resources.

Limits – Action
Our action plans need to work within the limits or overcome them, otherwise they will be unrealistic and unfulfilled.

The multiple faces of limits – Laura Bouwman, the Netherlands/France

Working with limits in my design for self-care brought me three learnings. Firstly, that adding solutions thinking to this anchor point paved the way for meaningful **ideas** and **action**. Adding this entails reflecting on how each limit can be a resource for change. For example, my **vision** centralised restoration of mental and physical health. However, health issues limited my usual physical exercise which frustrated me. The shift to viewing this limit as a resource made me realise that I can shift to soft, self-caring ways of stress-relief such as Kundalini yoga. This realisation led to incorporating such practices in **ideas** and became part of **action**.

Secondly, I learnt that limiting beliefs may require a kind approach rather than criticising myself for them. During designing, I found that my belief of 'only working hard makes me a good (enough), valuable person' made me feel guilty when taking time for self-care. Such beliefs are however common and may result from our cultural upbringing as well as broader societal cultural messages. A kind, caring strategy that I applied was to investigate whether these beliefs are true, and if not, let them go.

A last learning is that diving deep into limits may bring 'root-limits' to the surface that require taking responsibility for limits and perhaps even drastic change. Such deep diving may involve reflecting on 'why' a limit is actually a limit. In my design, I realised the high-pace, quantity oriented culture at my work as a limit for self-care. But asking why this is a limit redirected me to my 'working hard' belief. Yes, this belief is rooted in work-culture but I also actively contribute to it. Taking responsibility means that I either have to fight this culture or more drastically, leave work.

Limits also inspired my reflections on the process. I realised that my tendency is to get addicted to design work and not stop in time. My inner designer obviously also holds the belief that 'only working hard will do'. This exhausts me, even when engaged in something I really love. From now on, I aim to be a care-full designer, fostering energy and enthusiasm by taking many moments of self-care. Also, feedback from Looby made me aware that I tend to focus on limits and spirals of erosion, but shifting attention to what I wish to grow may further fuel motivation and gratitude. The multiple faces of limits allow for indicating what and how to grow, making this an unmissable anchor point.

PATTERNS

Places to visit

Our lives are an interwoven complex web of seen and unseen patterns. Intertwining patterns of work, play, eating, exercise, connecting, feeling, thinking. Some we have chosen, but others have just appeared almost by accident, and are then reinforced through repetition. For example, when we move house and a table gets put in a place maybe just because we were tired of carrying it and there was an available space, 10 years later we might wonder about its position and decide to move it; in the same way some patterns come into our lives by accident. Or some patterns served us well in the past but are now outdated with new contexts in our lives.

Revisiting our childhood can give us insights into the origin of these patterns. Any time when we are over or under doing something, such as overeating and underexercising, it is an opportunity for us to explore how to bring more balance in. Addictions are an overdoing of certain patterns.

Patterns invited us to go exploring in the boggy places, underground and underwater, to discover what is happening below the surface. Observation and self-awareness are our key attributes to take with us while exploring patterns. Pattern awareness is cultural awareness.

SYNCHRONISE WITH NATURAL PATTERNS AND CYCLES is an obvious invitation to weave the natural rhythms of the day, season and moon into our designs.

It takes time to repattern and build new habits. Make it a pattern to visit patterns.

Tools and methods for exploring

- Diaries
- Biotime logs (Recording natural phenomena over multiple years to see when things occur in relation to other things, and whether they are happening earlier or later than other years. This could be used for your own patterns, to see relationships between your eating, sleeping and other patterns over shorter timescales.)
- Nature's patterns
- Metaphors
- Transferable skills – what are your own patterns of effectiveness in other areas of your life?
- Ask other people about their patterns of success.
- Observing limiting beliefs or unhelpful thinking patterns.
- Digging deeper into patterns rather than the details, e.g. of arguments, internal conflicts, mood swings.
- 8 Shields model (see page 112).

Wisdom from the more-than-human world

Be like a snake and shed the skin of old patterns

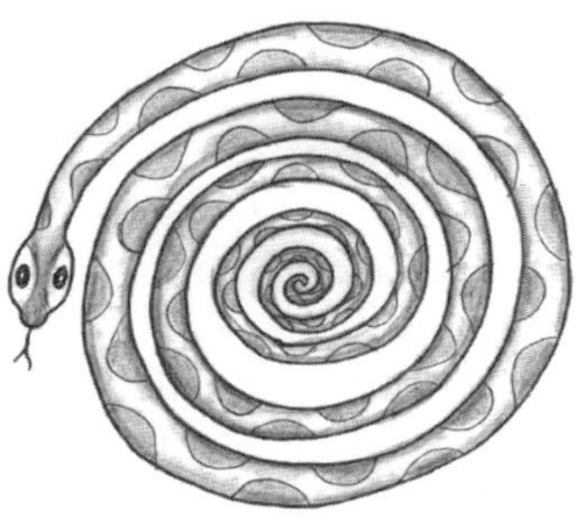

All of the more-than-human world could be emblematic of the patterns anchor point, because the patterns of life are universal and repeating in different forms throughout nature, including ourselves. The antlers of a deer have the same branching pattern as the trees, our lungs and the river systems. Spirals are repeated in snails, flowers, worms, shells, ferns, sunflowers.

If we are wanting to focus on growth, nature is full of real life examples of slow growth, rapid growth, incremental growth, non-linear growth and steady growth; we can find the metaphor that resonates with us and our design.

The more-than-human being that I would say chose me, rather than I chose it, is the snake. Over the years at Applewood we had seen grass snakes only twice before, and then while drawing the CEED deck two different grass snakes showed themselves to me. One was literally on my path up to my studio. I realised that they have many patterns within them: the spiral of their bodies curling round, and wave as they move, the tessellating pattern of their scales. And of course they have the perfect metaphor of shedding their skin as a reminder for ourselves to let go of old patterns.

Embodiment

Patterns become stored in our bodies; this can be helpful, such as muscle memory that enables us to ride a bike even after many years. It can also be unhelpful, such as repeating injuries. Patterns of thinking can lead us into mental loops. With new patterns slow steps start the process.

To embody the feeling of patterns, walk around in a spiral, outwards and then inwards.

Avoid

Patterns often become invisible to us, they just become 'the way we've always done something' if anyone asks, and often aren't even thought about this much. They are taken for granted, the status quo, assumed to be unbreakable.

Avoid replacing one unhelpful pattern with another, such as when giving up smoking to take up overeating or drinking. Or 'throwing out the baby with the bathwater' and letting go of useful patterns.

Some patterns are like quicksand and the more you try and get out of them, the deeper you go, such as arguing.

Cultural awareness

With patterns it is good to take cultural awareness with you. Every pattern you have has grown with multiple cultural contexts. For example, the amount you eat is relational to the parameters of cultural norms within your family and other cultures, all the way to the macro cultures of industrial cultures. In that context we might not think we are overeating but if we were to compare our calorie intake to hunter gatherers we would be way above their daily average. The hours of a day spent on phones is substantially more than a decade ago. With this in mind it is worth questioning all our patterns and trying to extract them as much as possible from these cultural contexts and see them for themselves. Is this the right amount for me, rather than, is this a 'normal' amount? TEND TO YOUR PERSONAL CULTURE principle directs us to focus on our patterns, to see them as our own unique complex web and encourages us to water our healthy habits, and weed out our unhelpful patterns.

Liberate and discover

PATTERN DISRUPTION is an essential part of change. You cannot have change without reweaving some of your patterns. Patterns is an opportunity to reflect and use your imagination to see the different picture you want to step into. It is also a chance to celebrate and nurture healthy patterns.

Through the patterns anchor point we discover ourselves and new ways of being. We are gifted with self-awareness and the ability to choose our patterns.

Weave and dance

Patterns – Momentum
Patterns are connected with momentum and creating routines for tending.

Patterns – Helps
Healthy patterns are helps, they support our growth.

Patterns – Limits
Unhelpful patterns are limits, with incremental
erosion and movement away from our vision.

Surfacing patterns as a container for health – Keira Oliver, Scotland

Learning about patterns in my systems change work has been such a liberating experience. They provide structure and flow, rather than when working at a detailed level which can throw up intense feelings of uncertainty and overwhelm. Observing patterns enables me to distance my own personal 'stuff' so I can be curious about what might be going on under the surface. What is playing out within my own body, family or team are often the same patterns and dynamics that are playing out in my wider systems.

My design to support my bad back to return to a more healthy place was all about patterns. I have had lower back pain, on occasion, throughout my adult life. It is usually instigated by heavy manual work combined with a particularly stressful time. The pain would last about a week and then ease up with little intervention. However, I then went through a period of intense debilitating pain on and off, followed by back issues for almost a year. When I plotted how much pain I was in each month, it suggests a pattern of increasing pain intensity and duration over time. The pattern had changed so I had to.

I used the Design Web when I was in an acute stage of pain. It surfaced some interesting patterns I hadn't been fully conscious of: I wasn't doing what I knew helped; resting was difficult, I ignored preceding niggles of pain, and often pushed through the pain so I didn't let people down. Something deeper was going on: what was my body trying to tell me?

I used a tool called Immunity to Change[1] to surface patterns of what might be keeping me stuck. This framework helps you explore why you might be resisting a certain change, even when you really want it, by identifying unconscious beliefs and assumptions, and hidden and competing commitments. It takes some deep reflection but can help you develop some strategies to address the 'immunity'. This uncovered that I had been living in survival mode for a long time due to a lot of changes in my life and work over a short period. I also noticed a misalignment between my mind, 'I have to keep going', with body, 'Something is not right here' and soul, 'What am I doing all this for?!' I had a whole set of potential designs as a result and had to discern which one would be the most helpful at this stage.

Integrating my observations, I decided to use the patterns as a structure: aligning mind, body and soul and shifting my behaviour across three phases. These were Managing (when in acute pain), Recovery, and Prevention. I relapsed towards the end of the project, but by putting my actions into practice, the acute stage lasted only three days – the shortest period of intense pain yet. As I write, nearly three months later, I still have discomfort and some pain with my back but I have not experienced another acute setback.

1 Kegan, R., & Lahey, L. L. (2009). *Immunity to Change.* Harvard Business Review Press

IDEAS

Places to visit

You will find yourself having ideas as soon as you step into a design, or even before. Have a page in your notebook or paper on your fridge, or a whiteboard in your office to capture ideas when they come.

In addition to catching ideas as they appear, pay an extended visit to the ideas anchor point with the intention of generating many more. Quantity is the aim rather than quality. There is no commitment to following through with any of them at this stage. The more adventurous and unusual, the more we are able to shake up our usual thoughts and discover new ways.

The principle STEP INTO THE UNKNOWN invites us to move outside our usual parameters for ideas. Challenge yourself and others to jump way outside these parameters into the ridiculous. From this there might be a small seed of possibility that couldn't have arisen otherwise. Your imagination is your key tool here. Take a big basket for harvesting all the ideas and aim to fill it.

As well as the imaginative, creative process, a more systematic research approach could be taken. Look at how other people have done things, researching on the internet, visiting other projects, asking experts.

Tools and methods for exploring

- Research
- Ask others, especially children
- Imagine being a hobbit, oak tree, penguin, alien, frog, toddler, elder
- Magician's wheel – in a group of people, have two circles of people facing each other in pairs. The inner circle are the magicians. The outer circle asks the magicians for ideas about something. They do not give any of the stories or **limits** behind this, they just ask a simple question like, please give me ideas for remembering songs/bringing more creativity into my life/having less arguments? The inner circle of magicians give as many ideas as they think of (without asking any questions). After a minute or two the inner circle moves round to another magician and asks again. This can continue until everyone has seen each of the magicians if you have time. The inner and outer circle then swap over, and the outer circle become the magicians and the inner circle ask their questions.
- Random assembly – place different elements on cards, then have a pile of prepositions. Pick two elements and one preposition, explore the idea that comes even if it feels ridiculous at first, such as a rabbit hutch on top of a greenhouse.

Do this many times with different combinations, think about how each idea could work. This frees us up to think of more unusual ideas.

- Use your subconscious mind – daydream, write ideas upon waking
- Stream of consciousness writing or talking
- Do an activity that involves both sides of your brain and then brainstorm ideas.

Wisdom from the more-than-human world

Go for quantity of ideas; like flowers not all ideas will set seed

The flower garden is our representation here of the varied abundance of ideas. Flowers come in all sorts of shapes, sizes and colours. They attract attention and give us joy to look at them. Not all flowers will become seeds or fruit, and not all seeds will go on to grow, but many will. Some will provide us with juiciness and nourishment, others will take time to become future generations of plants. The future plants won't be identical to their parents but will grow in their own way.

Embodiment

Imagine having many lightbulb moments – flashes of inspiration – and then collecting them in a basket. There is vitality and excitement and childlike curiosity and fun when you are fully in the creative flow of generating ideas. There is a widening of our viewpoints moving away from tunnel focus and expanding into new possibilities.

The movement here is the repetitive motion of collecting light bulbs or perhaps picking apples and putting them in our basket of ideas.

Avoid

Leave behind your realism filters. Put aside the part of your brain that wants to ask questions about whether it is possible, how long it will take to do it, who will object, who will help, whether you will be able to maintain it etc. All of these questions are relevant at other times, but while in the ideas stage we need to leave behind our questioning mind. When someone else shares a suggestion it is easy to come in with a quick 'no', or 'but', or immediately see the flaws and challenges with the idea. Instead just use it as a springboard for more of your own ideas.

Cultural awareness

We are generally not encouraged to be wild with our imaginings. There is a fear of judgement and rejection if we suggest something that isn't thought through carefully. We get trapped into our usual ways of thinking.

Liberate and discover

When encouraged to think outside of the box, we start noticing the box. What is the box that we are thinking within? What are the constraints of time, money, skills, values? What do we think is impossible but could become possible if we had the confidence, expertise, motivation, support... The box might be a more literal one, like being able to think outside of our home. By letting go of all of these and stepping further and further into the ideas anchor point, our imagination is freed. We connect with our inner child. We discover our playfulness and creativity.

Weave and dance

Ideas – Principles
Run ideas through the filter of principles and ethics, to decide which ones to take forward into integration.

Ideas – Action
After the abundance of ideas, we can visit action to see how the ideas might fit into the timeframes we have available to us.

Ideas – Limits
Many of our ideas will not be compatible with the limits we have.

Unfolding creativity – Louise Leisemei Paustian, Denmark

For my first diploma project, I chose to collaborate with a team of three. Our goal was to conceptualise and execute an extraordinary plant-based dining event in partnership with The Danish Green Youth Movement (DGUB), which had recently released its second book and manifesto focused on reclaiming nature and reimagining food systems.

We had various partners involved: Østre Gasværk Theatre as our venue (a large theatre in central Copenhagen), the climate-themed play Urinetown, DGUB, a distinguished moderator, and the two manifestos, alongside our emphasis on permaculture and food systems.

I found the circular structure of the Design Web particularly beneficial. Although I had only utilised it a handful of times before, I navigated through the anchor points while facilitating a workshop with three participants who were unfamiliar with both the Design Web and permaculture.

Arriving at **limits** we quickly realised that we had many partners and, therefore, many messages that needed to be made understandable and clear.

In my experience, group brainstorming often leads to a flurry of fragmented ideas, often diverging in unexpected directions without necessarily contributing to a cohesive vision.

However, having our **limits** clear and focusing on the ideas anchor point truly transformed our experience. As newcomers to the Design Web, we progressed methodically from **vision** to **ideas**, allowing us to establish clear boundaries and work through **helps**, **limits**, and **patterns**. Upon reaching ideas we experienced a surge of creativity that birthed concepts we hadn't previously imagined. It felt like the anchor point allowed creativity to flow freely, akin to water, enabling ideas to emerge and interconnect into a unified whole.

We came up with many bold ideas, which we later had to abandon when revisiting **limits** and **patterns**. In this way, we realised that by spending time understanding what both supports and constrains the project, we were better able to stress-test all ideas and ensure they were feasible and sustainable.

I therefore experienced that not only did we come up with better and more ideas, but the process as a group was also more enjoyable and easier when it came to making the right decisions that led to the best outcome.

As a designer and creative soul, I have always thrived in generating ideas and immersing myself in creative processes. However, finding tools that help structure and align creativity has been transformative. Working with the Design Web has provided a framework to channel my ideas effectively, ensuring they align with **vision** and contribute meaningfully to the bigger picture. This approach has enhanced my ability to design regenerative and resilient events, processes, and projects, making the creative journey more cohesive and impactful. It's a process that combines inspiration with structure, resulting in solutions that are both innovative and sustainable.

PRINCIPLES

Places to visit

Principles are guidance for our adventure. They have arisen from observation of best practices, underlying attitudes and fundamental wisdom. There are many principles in life, each subject and skill area will have some: knowledge about carpentry, cooking, sport, teaching, gardening, nursing. These gems of wisdom are part of the inheritance of humanity that is passed from generation to generation and refined each time. Principles appear as sayings, adages, proverbs, affirmations, reminders, mottos. Permaculture principles originally arose from indigenous wisdom and observation of nature. The Cultural Emergence principles arose from observations, conversations, poetry, designs and deep thought.

Sprinkle principles throughout. They will give us different information depending on where we are on our adventure. At the beginning they give us a springboard and the impetus to get started. Later they help us navigate choices as they arise. They anchor our intentions and support our actions in different ways as we progress. The principles help us discern ways of navigating unfolding emergent properties. USE EMERGENCE TO SUPPORT EMERGENCE speaks to this ongoing unfurling of the design.

They are used in conjunction with other anchor points to encourage more exploration and highlight key issues. The principle RECEIVE ENCOURAGEMENT might guide us to ask others about our qualities and add more to the **helps** anchor points, for example. The principles serve as threads weaving our design together.

Principles are signposts directing us to more Earth care, people care and fair shares. They bring us more into alignment with our **vision** and effective ways to act.

Principles bring nutrients of encouragement, flow and alignment. Nutrients that help our designs grow in strength and collaboration.

Tools and methods for exploring

- Pick them at random.
- Ask everyone to pick a principle for the group culture.
- Use the Cultural Emergence principles colouring book[1] to make posters.
- With a group, rotate people's colouring page, so that each person is adding to other ones, this is a great way of literally illustrating EMERGENCE HAPPENS IN RELATIONSHIP.
- Create guilds of principles that reinforce key messages.
- Make your own – what is a piece of distilled wisdom that you want to convey?

1 This is available free when you sign up for our newsletter www.cultural-emergence.com

- Ask experts for their principles.
- Create a table with your options across the top and different principles in the column, tick which principles correspond to which option. This will highlight the option that is aligned with the most principles.
- Choose a principle at the beginning of the day or week and observe it in action.
- Use them as reflective prompts or health checks for your life, group, design.

Wisdom from the more-than-human world

Be like the butterfly and embody the principles of emergence

All around us life is demonstrating emergence. There are a multitude of examples of emergence in the more-than-human world. Every being in nature has found their natural gifts and ways of expressing them. Principles remind us that we are nature, that we have all of these capabilities literally hardwired into our DNA, they are part of our blueprint of being human alive on Earth. The more-than-human world is the inspiration for growth, adaptation, interaction. Life is emergence: tadpoles becoming frogs, germinating seeds, flowers becoming juicy fruit.

The butterfly is the representation here as the archetypal example of emergence, the caterpillar turning to pupa and then to butterfly. It reminds us of radical transformation, letting go, flying free.

Embodiment

The movement is to look through a lens. Imagine the principles are giving you special powers of observation and insight. They magnify the solutions and possibilities for us. They also act as a filter, removing the dust of indecision and unethical choices. They support us to act with decisiveness, anchoring us to our chosen pathways.

Avoid

Principles are not dogma or rules. Do not think that they represent universal, absolute truths that must be obeyed, there are exceptions. Don't get too attached to them or take them to unhelpful extremes. Avoid using them as retorts to others, or ways of pointing out their faults. Avoid trying to use all of them at once; this can lead to overwhelm and lose the potency of finding ones that fit well.

Cultural awareness

Each culture has its own principles, messages and proverbs. These are a reflection of cultural priorities and values. The principles often point to common sense which is no longer common in our world.

Liberate and discover

The principles act as keys to unlock our thinking. Over time we become more fluent in the language of them. We observe them in daily life; they come to mind when we meet challenges. When groups use them regularly they arise naturally in conversation. This increasing fluency is an indicator. With different sets of principles they will be indicators of different things, such as sustainability or health. Cultural Emergence principles are indicators of connection, community, creativity, emergence, flow, encouragement and excitement.

Weave and dance

Principles – Momentum
The principles keep us on track and support us to build momentum.

Principles – Reflection
Reflect on progress using the principles.

Principles – Vision
The principles help us to find and refine our vision,
ensuring it is in line with our ethics and values.

Invitations to a deeper listening – Helene Bøhler, Norway/Scotland

When I design, one thing I look for is the quality of what I want to nurture. This quality is often expressed in one of the principles and helps anchor my focus. Integrating Passion and Work-expression was a design for an introduction to permaculture workshop. I identified TRUST THE PROCESS as one of the central principles, and this served as a reminder both throughout my planning, and during the workshop itself. It helped me to listen to how to stay connected to myself in trust, and also to invite more flow when I was in implementation and connecting with participants at the workshop.

I love the fun and inspiring journey of listening for the principle(s) that speak most clearly about the essence. Like a recurring reminder, I find the principles act as a mantra to keep listening for the quality and feeling of what I am engaged in, to support my connection, focus and direction.

On my diploma, as a practitioner and teacher of Tai Chi, as an artist and in life in general, I feel supported and inspired by the deeper listening that principles invite. This anchor point acts as a bridge and keeps returning me to connection with nature, universal truths and human ecology.

For example, in my design called Space for Emergence, this principle acts as a reminder to listen for spaciousness and allow for something unplanned to arise. In this case, having named this after a specific principle, it holds a very central role. And it is exactly because I find this principle so inspiring and central to my needs that I have given it such a focus.

My intention is to create a dedicated time in my week for 'no plans' and to see what arises (i.e. space for emergence), in this time. However a key experience has been that while I have been listening for how and when to create this dedicated golden time in my week, the quality LEAVE SPACE FOR EMERGENCE has instead become infused in my life. And so the need has been met by allowing for emergence and not necessarily just 'sticking to the plan'.

I love that the principles are open-ended guides. And with the openness they invite, they are in line with life's mystery. When I think of designing, I often think of 'planning'. However, it is more than making plans; it is also about how to make myself 'adventure prone' – being receptive to the unexpected events in life. Responding to changes, while staying rooted. Like nature I move organically into life, and as a designer, I aim to enhance the flow and effectiveness by aligning with life. The principles support that alignment.

INTEGRATION

Places to visit

Integration is where all the magic happens. Something happens in the integration anchor point that is beyond the insights that occur in the other ones. It brings together creative flow, big picture thinking and pragmatism. There is an alchemy of all the information harvested so far, plus an extra sprinkling of emergence and synchronicity. Integration reveals a clear focus and elevates it to the next level.

Sometimes it seems like a mysterious magic trick, where you don't quite know what is happening, but suddenly it's like the tablecloth is whisked away from under the plates, and the design appears in front of us. At times though, it seems like just a big mess of ingredients with no idea what it is going to bake. And we have to lean into the principle of TRUST THE PROCESS.

At times the needs are obvious from early on, and then we have the joy of bringing it together with ideas of how to meet those needs and how it all connects. The whole process can be seen as – you have *this*, you want *that* and you collect ideas of how to bridge the gap. In integration you make decisions. The needs are the gaps to fill – the things that would move us forward to manifesting our vision if we manage to meet them. What are we trying to achieve? We ask ourselves, what are the important things that the design needs to do and how do we do them?

This involves synthesis, distillation, commitment and decision making. It requires us to be focused, grounded, analytical and decisive. Integration is fundamental to success and realisation. It is a process of collecting and reordering information, bringing new connections and meaning.

Integration is the place where the adventure comes into a cohesive whole. This happens over a few visits. There is a convergence and divergence rhythm between integration and all the other anchor points.

The first part is to gather our needs, which come from digesting our observations, enquiries and activities of the other anchor points. I use the terms needs and functions interchangeably. What are the functions to fulfil?

Learning to identify needs as you go is a fast track to effective designing. When you get to grips with doing this then your creativity and thought goes to how to meet those needs. At first though it will make more sense to go back through the anchor points specifically with this question in mind. This brings a convergence of needs into integration.

Frame your needs as verbs, something that is active and you are doing, such as increasing, decreasing, creating, building, enhancing, developing, improving, embracing, connecting, allowing, supporting, producing, releasing, strengthening, rewriting, growing, shifting. Cluster your needs into themes, such as being/doing, work/play, inner/outer. Are there any themes that are emerging? You might be able to pick out some key functions and then supporting functions, e.g. generating income is a key need, marketing is a supporting function. Sometimes the grouping comes first and then can be explored deeper to find the supporting needs. Other times the whole collection of needs appears and then we categorise them.

Next, when you have your needs, it is time to go exploring again in the other anchor points for pragmatic and creative solutions. The main source for this will be in **ideas**. It is also a chance to revisit your **vision** and see if there is more to add. This is the divergence and exploratory stage.

The ways we meet needs can be referred to as systems or elements. Systems are related objects, methods, people that together fulfil one of the functions; the elements are the individual components.

The second visit to integration is when you return with your ideas, coming back into the convergence rhythm. Deciding which of the wild ideas you want to bring home and tame. It is a process of prioritising and selecting the most appropriate ones. The ones that you feel are compatible with the information from the other anchor points. Do they make use of your **helps**? Will they create helpful **patterns**? Are they within realistic cultural **limits**? Will they take you towards your **vision**? Do they make a realistic **action** plan? Are you able to maintain these systems and build **momentum**? This selection process involves commitment, if you aren't committed to an idea then it is best to leave it in the **ideas**, you can always come back to it at a later stage. From this you will see patterns emerging. You take the good ideas and shape them into something new. The principle WEAVE UNITY illustrates how, with weaving all of these needs and systems for meeting the needs, you are building a holistic design.

Optimising systems

After selecting them, the next step is to optimise the systems and look for synergies and flows between them. The permaculture principle of 'every system meets multiple needs' reminds us that there is the potential to get more yields out of the same inputs and actions. This can help in our decision-making processes. For instance, if one of our needs is for exercising, there are many forms this could take. Joining a walking club means we could meet the needs of exercising, building community and connecting with the more-than-human world simultaneously. So one system meets many needs.

This weaving together of systems has the potential to connect things that weren't connected before. This process can lead to elegant complexity, where the layers interact and create harmonious relationships. It is a time where emergent properties arise, with unexpected yields and exchanges.

There is also the potential for elegant simplicity, where simple, easy, effective solutions show themselves. Where the answers are effortless. One example of this was on a course where we decided to start each session with silence until everyone had arrived. It solved the issues around late arrivals, giving people more space to themselves, and me having time to focus my energies for the coming session, all in a couple of minutes of doing nothing – that is elegant simplicity!

You also want to use the permaculture principle, have 'multiple back ups', and have different ways of meeting each need, especially the key needs. So in the previous example, having several ways to exercise, connect with the more-than-human world and build community. Using both of these principles leads us to a web of reinforcing, interconnected systems within our designs. Drawing a circle with all the needs and/or systems around the outside and then drawing lines between them helps you see existing and potential connections.

We may not know all the ways in which we can meet our needs at the start. When we know our needs though, they become a useful checklist when a new idea, project, invitation, request or opportunity comes up. Identifying the needs allows us to be observant in life in a new way, and then opportunities arise that might have otherwise been overlooked. It is an exciting part as pathways appear and there is a sense it is actually going to happen.

One or more of the key needs that you identify might seem so pivotal that you want to take them forward into a design of their own. When you have a few designs going in your life you can start to weave between them as well.

There may be a few pulses of this convergence and divergence before you feel the emergence of your design.

The final stage of integration is to create a representation. This is your portal to all the thinking you have done. It is fun and empowering, and the design comes to life before our eyes in a very literal sense. It is something for you to keep present in your daily life. It could be a drawing or painting, collage, affirmation, photograph, sculpture, embroidery, item of clothing, poem, song, mandala, symbol, mantra, mind map, story. Whatever it is, when you keep it handy and within sight and reach, you are much more likely to keep your design alive than if you just put it in a drawer or on a shelf.

Integration gives a sense of groundedness, and a 'can do, will do' feeling. With other people, there is a sense of relief when everyone is clear about the needs. People have agency, direction and accountability for meeting those needs.

Tools and methods for exploring

- The five year old 'Why?' To help identify needs, repeatedly ask yourself why? Why do I want to do this? Why is this a limit? Find the reasons behind the ideas.
- Tables of needs and systems
- Draw a web of connections – how are the elements connected with each other?
- Inputs and outputs – what does each system give and receive?
- Artwork
- Flow diagrams
- Maps

Wisdom from the more-than-human world

Be like the spider weaving your design thinking into an interconnected whole

The spider weaving is the image that clearly expresses this anchor point. There is beauty in all weaving. Spiders weave many webs, a reminder for us to not just do one design but continually weave new ones. Weave a web and then see what it catches. Be observant for vibrations on the web alerting you to changes and yields.

Embodiment

The movement is bringing your hands together, fingers intertwined. A sense of bringing it all together as a whole. The sense in your body is one of decisiveness and effectiveness. It might not feel like this at first, often there is a period of confusion to go through before the fog lifts and you see distant horizons. A feeling of pieces slotting into place happens here.

Avoid

Avoid getting ahead of yourself in the process, and thereby confusing yourself. Take it step by step and the tangled wool will become a beautiful weave.

Avoid overcomplexity. It is a complex process, but sometimes the answers are right there in front of you, hiding in plain view.

It is easy to get attached to a strategy or system for meeting a need, rather than thinking of the need itself.

Cultural awareness

There is a predominance of reductionist thinking. Instead of seeing many contributing factors and layered and intersecting problems, there is a tendency to examine problems in isolation. This same thinking is then applied to finding solutions, and working in silos, instead of finding solutions that integrate and answer many issues at once.

Liberate and discover

Through integration, we discover cohesion and find solutions. We discover our gifts as systems thinkers, sensing interconnections between things. It is an expression of our creative genius as humans to bring things together to create new wholes.

Weave and dance

Integration receives information and sends out connections to every other anchor point.

Integration – Vision
What are the needs to help us reach our vision? Imagine yourself with all these needs met, take time to add to your vision.

Integration – Limits
Flip your limits into needs, ways to decrease or overcome your limits, or grow things that you are lacking.

Integration – Helps – Appreciation
Visit helps to find support for meeting needs, and appreciation to acknowledge all the ways our needs are already being met.

Integration – Reflection – Patterns
How and when have these needs been met in the past?
Can you identify unhelpful and helpful patterns?

Integration – Ideas – Principles
Visit ideas to bring in some creative, imaginative, divergent thinking.
What are the multitude of ways we can meet our needs?
Then check your ideas with the principles.

Integration – Action – Momentum
Next we need to know when and how to set up these systems and how to maintain them.

Integration – Pause
What are the needs from pause?
What are the fun, regenerative ways of meeting needs?

Weaving the magic – Looby Macnamara, UK

I have noticed when teaching the Design Web, that it takes a little while for people to understand integration. Perhaps because we are so used to jumping to something we think we need, instead of trying to understand what we actually need. How often might we say 'I need chocolate'? Chocolate isn't a need in itself, it's a way of meeting needs, which might be various, such as comfort, energy, a pause or perhaps even the need for food. In that way chocolate might actually be quite a good synergistic satisfier. Although at times it is a pseudo satisfier and there could be better, healthier ways of meeting those needs.

Once people grasp finding needs, then everything else flows: creativity, opportunities, synchronicities. Our problem solving brain is activated, which of course is different for everyone. For me, I enjoy doing jigsaw puzzles, and I feel this is what is happening, the picture is coming together, and there is a sense of satisfaction when a piece falls into place. Sometimes I already have a feeling of what the picture is that I am trying to create, other times it is quite mysterious at first. I also think of it as the alchemical process of cooking, although at times the adage, 'you can't make an omelette without breaking eggs' comes to mind, and it feels like a messy process.

For other people I have noticed that they find their own ways with integration. Some in a very structured way, others in a more organic way. It's always intriguing to observe. For myself it depends on the type of design. If it is something that I have planned many times before, such as a course, there is a familiar pattern, and the needs are clear and then I get creative with ways to bring them in. I create a table with the functions and all the systems to meet them. And then I cross reference this with the sessions to ensure that there is a balance across the whole course. For example, connection to nature is met just by being here at Applewood, and within different sessions, or checking that there is a balance between time for learning with each other, and self reflection time, and teaching time. If it is a new type or something a bit more abstract then it takes me a little longer to find the needs, but when I do there is a satisfying clarity and direction.

For my Regenerative Arm Movement design, some of the needs were posture, fun things to do with my arms, restorative sleep, releasing tension, using and training my left arm and exercise. Going deeper into the need of exercise I identified needs of exercise to strengthen, to stretch, to loosen; each of these had different options and solutions. Knowing what I was needing helped me to find appropriate solutions, and I realised that yoga actually supports a lot of the needs all at once.

Within my Becoming a Songleader design I discovered that I had a need for remembering that I know songs *and* to overcome that blank feeling when someone asks if anyone has a song. For this I created a song pouch which has little cards with all the songs I know on them. This was my representation of the whole design, as well as meeting this particular need.

As you might expect I did many designs for writing this book. One of them was for the week ahead when I had just one week to go. For **reflection** on the previous week one of my thorns was feeling quite overwhelmed, and having a lot of thoughts along the lines of 'it's too much'. Then in **vision** the three qualities I chose were creative, focused and cheerful. In **limits**, I wanted to minimise any negative self-talk. This led me to making positive self-talk one of my primary needs. I realised that this was the golden key. It was very simple, but without it I could easily descend into a spiral of erosion – where stress leads to lack of creativity leads to being further behind leads to more stress. Instead I was able to intervene with this spiral with my affirmation 'stay cheerful'. I reframed deadlines to lifelines and was looking forward to the freedom that was coming just before my birthday, rather than feeling the dread of a deadline. I created a spiral of productivity where enjoying it led to more flow and led to feeling on top of things. Through this affirmation I managed to weather the literal storms with snow, ice and then flooding that also came our way that week.

Within the Cultural Emergence Going Global design, the needs fitted into three categories – creating a toolkit, raising the profile of Cultural Emergence and creating networks of people using the toolkit. From knowing these needs, the priorities became obvious. After creating the toolkit, attention turned to creating networks. One of the ways is through the online community space; this became another design. The needs for the community were grouped into creating a connected team culture and effective project management of running the community; creating content to share; bringing people into the community; and encouraging participation and connection. Each of these needs could become a design in itself with further detail, and they are all interconnected and a part of the whole community design; there are designs within designs.

Although very different, all of these have the same sense within integration, the feelings of it making sense, coming together, flowing into one cohesive stream.

ACTION

Places to visit

This is the place where our design becomes real through our actions. As people we are used to doing, but sometimes that just results in feelings of busyness without the sense of achievement and productivity. We feel like hamsters on a wheel just going round in circles. Instead here, we ground it in strategic thought, so that we know each action is moving us towards our **vision**. It is a chance to connect with **helps** and ensure that we have the resources for the job, or clarity over what else we need.

This anchor point is the edge between thinking about doing, and getting on and doing it. We need to make plans so that our actions are strategic and well thought through. But we can't always see all that is needed to reach our **vision**. We might need to start and make the first steps to then be able to see around the corner.

Action helps us to make mistakes on paper. The sequencing and dependencies become visible. Any clashes of commitment are highlighted and work reevaluated.

MOVE THE TOOLS reminds us that manifestation only comes when we move the relevant tools.

Tools and methods for exploring

- Timelines
- Calendars
- Lists
- Flow diagrams
- Spreadsheets or tables with who, what, when, how and how long each task will take
- Mind maps
- Divide tasks into – now, soon and later
- Paint a river of activity and add post-it notes
- SMART goals (Specific, Measurable, Achievable, Realistic, Timely)
- Post-it notes for each action
- Big pieces of paper on the wall with tasks for each week before an event

Wisdom from the more-than-human world

Become a busy and effective bee

Bees are known for their capacity to work hard. While they might look like they are expending a lot of energy flying around, it is not aimless activity. They are strategic and have clear intentions. They only visit flowers that are open. In fact, with new scientific discovery it is shown that there is communication between the flowers and pollinators, with flowers emitting a different light when they have already been visited so that the bees don't waste time going to a flower without pollen.

Action is a way for us to map out our flight path strategically.

Embodiment

The movement for action is running. Have a quick run, feel the energy in your body. This is the sense here, the movement brings energy and vitality. There is a flow to our actions. We literally end up in a different place to where we started.

Avoid

Our action plans often go off course, with unforeseen limits and new opportunities arising. It is good to avoid the temptation to then think that the action plan is obsolete and useless and there is no point in revisiting it. That is exactly the time to readjust the action plan. Leave behind your feelings of 'not enough' and guilt and stress if things aren't going according to the plan.

Equally avoid sticking rigidly to the plan; this may lead to burnout or missed opportunities. PLAN THEN FLOW is a reminder that planning is important, but then we need to flow with what is actually happening and needs and opportunities that arise.

Cultural awareness

We live in a very task oriented society, where doing is valued over being. Often there is consumption with action, fossil fuels and resources are used, waste is created. There is a glorification of being busy. This busyness isn't necessarily in the direction of the ethics or our vision though. Instead of saying I am busy, I like to say I am being productive, or we could say we are maximising our potential.

We all have different styles of adventuring, some of us like to have a complete schedule for our journey, others like to just begin and see what happens. When we are designing with other people it is useful to share our different styles. Bringing those patterns into the open and sharing with our collaborators is useful. This will support us to be more empathetic with each other.

Liberate and discover

Creating an action plan is an empowering way of seeing how your vision will become reality. Through our actions we build confidence in our abilities. Create patterns of success through commitment to small achievable steps and following through with them.

The Greeks had two different words for time, Kronos and Kairos. Kairos timing is a different way of feeling for the opportune moment, rather than Kronos timing which is governed by the clock. Kairos timing invites us to attune our body to our actions, feeling into when things need doing and when we have capacity for them. At the right time, when we are in the right mood, actions flow effortlessly. Within the action anchor point we lay out the tasks needed and think about when but we don't need to be wedded to it as the only way, time or sequence that things happen. Remain observant for the moments when something feels like the right thing to do.

Weave and dance

Action – Vision
Revisit your vision as you will be able to see more detail
as you progress with your adventure.

Action – Momentum
Anything that we implement will need maintenance at times.
Check the maintenance plan is achievable before committing yourself.

Action – Helps
We need to know what resources we have available for each step in
our action plans. Resources of people, skills, energy, enthusiasm,
time, materials, tools are all important helps.

Making a dream come true – Bernard Joseph, France/Belgium

I'm a dreamer, an entrepreneur and a long distance runner. Most of my creative ideas, projects and problem solving come during running. My mind is stimulated by oxygen and breathing, by nature connection, and by movement. So action is sometimes a starting point for me to let new designs emerge. It is the place where a dream comes true, where ideas take shape in matter.

I use the Design Web every day, for very small designs to larger ones, such as translating *People & Permaculture* into French and building my home. Most of the time it stays in my head, and I review the anchor points in my mind. When it comes to action, something appears and comes to life. The implicit becomes explicit; the design starts to breathe in real life.

I like the idea that we shouldn't focus only on completion, but rather on enjoying the path with every step, instant by instant. For me, the purpose of the Design Web is also to bring abundance in our lives. It's the process of transforming ideas and dreams into useful and joyful realities.

In order to use action to its full potential, it must include resources from other anchor points which are necessary to actually make it real and come into life. For example, with building my house, I needed to know what kind of house I would like to build from **vision**, and what my **helps** are, in terms of money, time, tools, contractors, materials. I also need to know my **limits** in terms of legal regulations, neighbourhood, soil, accessibility. And it's useful to understand my **patterns** and how to transform my spiral of erosion into a spiral of abundance. In **ideas** I imagine all the lovely additional things I could include in my house. **Integration** will help me to check that all my personal and family needs are covered. **Principles** will support life on Earth and are also connected to **reflection** and **appreciation**.

From there I created my action plan on spreadsheets, both on computer and on a big board with post-its. On the top of the columns, I listed: Action Step; Resources in Time (Full-Time Equivalent in days/person); Resources in Money; Resources in Material; Limits; followed by a calendar planning (by day, week...). Then vertically, I listed all the actions and corresponding data. I used colours to fill it in across the planning, by coordinator or type of action, for example. At the bottom of the spreadsheet, I had the total cost and number of people needed each day or week to accomplish all the tasks.

Without the Design Web I wonder if I would have accomplished so many transformations in my life in the last decade. The Design Web is like an ancient tool, it's inspired by nature and empowers us to be creative and to support life on Earth.

MOMENTUM

Places to visit

Momentum is where we take care of our design. Through our regular tending our design grows, the ethics grow, our effectiveness grows. We make a plan for this pattern of care and attention, for the tasks that need doing on a daily, weekly, seasonal and annual basis. Implementation is one thing, it is another to keep what you have. Without maintenance something useful becomes useless.

There are two aspects to momentum, one is how to maintain what we set up, the regular tasks such as daily watering or ongoing social media. The other aspect is about building momentum. When we start out getting fit for example, maybe a 15 minute walk is plenty, but after a while, that will seem easy and we are ready for more. Part of momentum is recognising when something is going well and we are able to increase it. Momentum is built through creating patterns of success: starting small, lowering your expectations and then exceeding them.

Sometimes when I write up momentum with all that I need to do, I feel overwhelmed and then realise that I need to scale down. If we don't pay attention to momentum, the energy put in is lost. But when we do put attention into it, then surprising things can happen in the design and it can go to a whole new level. Honesty and foresight are needed at the beginning, so that it builds in a sustainable way, while leaving the possibility open that momentum may build in sudden, exponential, unexpected ways.

The principles WORK TO COMPLETION and BEAUTY IN COMPLETION invite us to build momentum through splitting tasks into manageable chunks and celebrating milestones. Create islands of beauty in your home and pockets of calm in your day. Maintain these and start to see how they might grow and connect with another island or pocket. Momentum supports you to keep connected and moving towards your **vision**.

Tools and methods for exploring

- Tables
- Maintenance charts
- Explore your momentum inhibitors and builders
- Rotas
- Graphs
- Map spirals of erosion and turn them into spirals of abundance – where instead of things getting steadily worse, they get incrementally better.

Wisdom from the more-than-human world

Unfurl like the fern, repeat your pattern of growth

In May and June each year at Applewood the ferns unfurl. They grow at an astonishing rate over the next few weeks. Their pattern of growth is fractal and it is through repetition that they find their way.

Embodiment

The movement is rocking back and forth, or side to side. Like being on a swing there can be either the steady rhythm that maintains our height or one of increasing rhythm, acceleration and gaining height. We need to keep the movement going or the swing stops. There is a sense of growth and movement in our bodies. It is a steadier movement than the running movement in **action**.

Feel the momentum swing in your body, the turning point when you feel the increasing flow towards your **vision**.

Avoid

Procrastination is the killer of momentum. When we put off the tasks that need doing they invariably get bigger – in our minds even if not in reality. The proverb 'a stitch in time saves nine' reminds us that the sooner we fix something the easier it is. When we procrastinate the jobs stack up and lead to overwhelm. When we don't maintain things they become energy drains, and time, energy and resources are wasted. It also drains our emotional energy and depletes our confidence.

It is important to not have so many things to maintain that you feel overwhelmed. Avoid false economies of starting projects that you don't have capacity to maintain.

Let go of tasks that become too costly in terms of time, energy, money, meetings to plan the tasks etc., and then get left undone, wasting away in our guilt pile. This will be counterproductive and decrease our capacities, energy and confidence. Achievability is the key to success with momentum. If it doesn't feel achievable, or if I don't do it then it is counterproductive, and I feel guilty and disempowered. If I do do it, then I am creating a pattern of success for myself.

Cultural awareness

The dominant fast paced culture gives more attention to shiny new things rather than valuing the old. We are constantly encouraged to discard and dispose of old things, and replace rather than repair them. A similar pattern is how funders want to fund new projects but not the ongoing running costs of charities. This is turning the paradigm of 'replace rather than repair' around to 'repair rather than replace'.

Liberate and discover

Momentum involves work, and work brings yields. The yields support more momentum. This anchor point requires us to access our stamina, trust and patience.

Growth can be non-linear with changing states, quantum leaps, evolution and emergence. Momentum can lead us to arrive in a different state of being and functioning. For example, instead of tidying and arriving again at the same place, we take it to a new level of being tidied, and we are now maintaining around this new norm.

Through momentum we gain traction towards our vision. Instead of seeing these tasks as chores or burdens, reframe them as joyful connections. See them as a way of honouring your vision and your commitment to it. Service is love in action.

Weave and dance

Momentum – Reflection
From observing momentum flows and blockages we
can reflect upon contexts that have contributed to them.

Momentum – Vision
As we build our momentum and grow our effectiveness,
our visions can grow, expand and be more ambitious.

Momentum – Limits
When we lose momentum, we need to visit limits and
see what is blocking our path, or draining our energy.

Breaking the cycle – Jelena Bozic, Serbia

When I started creating the *Everyday Permaculture Workbook*, I envisioned an accessible introduction to sustainable living practices, specifically tailored for everyday use. The main idea was to present permaculture in a way that resonates with the younger people in Serbia, moving beyond the common misconceptions of it being overly technical or solely about gardening.

The challenge I faced was not just about content creation but about sustaining the momentum required to bring this **vision** to life. Momentum became crucial to the success of this project. It provided the energy and direction often needed to overcome the common pitfalls, the same ones that hindered my previous projects.

After my first encounter with the Design Web, I realised that a significant reason some of my past projects failed was due to a lack of sustained energy and focus. Without enough momentum, the outcomes were often underwhelming, and the projects remained incomplete. However, understanding and harnessing the power of the momentum anchor point allowed me to break through this barrier.

The turning point came when I committed to dedicating at least one hour a day to creating the workbook. This consistency created a rhythm and a sense of progress that kept the project alive and moving forward. During this period of daily dedication, a synchronistic event occurred – a close friend reached out, offering to help with the project. This unexpected support not only fuelled the momentum but also brought fresh energy and ideas that were instrumental in shaping the final product.

This experience highlighted the magic of momentum. When you consistently invest time and energy, the universe seems to respond, bringing the right people and opportunities into your path. Momentum became more than just a concept; it was the driving force that transformed my **vision** into a tangible, impactful resource.

Through this process, I also discovered a deeper connection with my inner designer. The momentum I built didn't just move the project forward; it unlocked my creativity and allowed me to explore new ways of presenting permaculture. The workbook became more than just a collection of tips; it turned into a guide that inspires practical action, both physically and mentally, in everyday life. I am now finishing a project to turn it into a timeless calendar.

For me, momentum is not just about movement; it's about creating a sustained flow of energy that carries my design from concept to completion. It's about recognising the importance of small, consistent efforts and being open to the synchronicities that can help you along the way. This anchor point not only helped me complete the *Everyday Permaculture Workbook* but also deepened my understanding of how to bring regenerative practices to life in a way that is engaging and accessible to my local community.

APPRECIATION

Places to visit

The appreciation anchor point has two parts to it. The first is sharing your appreciation for all the things that support your design. The second is to think about how and when to build in ongoing regular times of appreciation.

Creating these regular times is a way of bringing **momentum**. It helps keep us in the present moment and abundance thinking, valuing what is here right now. As a regular practice we co-create a culture of appreciation as the foundation of our design culture.

Nothing builds a field of encouragement as strongly as appreciation of each other. Equally lack of appreciation erodes **momentum** and motivation. Activating the principles GIVE ENCOURAGEMENT and RECEIVE ENCOURAGEMENT generates a potent field for growth and support.

The principle of USE THE INTELLIGENCE OF CO-OPERATING HEARTS shares the power of a group when they use gratitude to come into a heart space. There is a deeper level of wisdom, trust and valuing. The collective power of the group increases exponentially.

Tools and methods for exploring

- Gratitude journal
- Self appreciation
- Choosing themes for appreciation such as nature, each other, food
- Gratitude for the past, and all the events leading us here, even the challenging times
- Writing or speaking appreciations to each other
- Starting emails with gratitude
- Starting meetings with a round of appreciation
- Taking an appreciation walk before starting designing together
- Whiteboard or noticeboard where people can write or doodle their gratitude of the day

Wisdom from the more-than-human world

Be like a dog, show appreciation for the small things

Dogs guide us into appreciation. A wagging tail is their archetypal expression of gratitude.

Our dog Baloo is happy at all the little things, happy to see us again, happy for the tiny biscuit treat, happy for the walk. Dogs repeatedly show appreciation for the same things, never taking it for granted that they will get fed again.

Embodiment

The movement is to place one hand on your heart and the other on your belly. Appreciation brings us into a heart space. Our hand on our belly is symbolic of gratitude for all the yields we gain from our adventure. Our yields may be the actual food for our belly, they may also be feeding us in different ways: our creativity, our sense of purpose, building our community and our friendships.

Avoid

We need to leave behind habits of complaining or self-depreciation. They are the complete opposite of what we are trying to do here. We also need to avoid the quagmire of 'not enoughness'.

Cultural awareness

For many indigenous cultures, thanksgiving comes before anything else. Starting with gratitude brings us into awareness of the interconnectedness of life. Our lives depend on the water, soil, trees, birds and bees. Appreciating each other also demonstrates that we are not lone wolves, but interdependent with each other.

In the modern world we have been conditioned away from appreciation, because we buy less things if we value what we have. Gratitude is an antidote to the capitalist paradigm. It is counter-cultural to appreciate ourselves, to celebrate our commitment, kindness, courage, playfulness, our smile and laughter, our skills.

Liberate and discover

With appreciation we come into a heart space. We are then more able to access our heart wisdom. Our heart wisdom comes from a gentle place of interconnectedness, of kindness, of ethics. Our nervous system is acting from a place of connection rather than disconnection. When we work with others coming into the heart space, this allows for a flow of connection, co-operation and heart wisdom. This heart space is an expansive place where we are filled with awe and wonder at the world and our place within it. More solutions and possibilities become available to us.

Gratitude helps us to acknowledge our privilege. When coming from a place of gratitude there is more capacity to find ways to LEVEL PRIVILEGE and give space for others to share and offer practical help and resources.

Even in challenging situations, appreciation helps us to seek support and find solutions or at least find acceptance. Gratitude builds resilience.

Weave and dance

Appreciation – Momentum
Appreciation is a momentum builder, encouraging everyone
to give their best, and ensuring people feel valued.

Appreciation – Patterns
Appreciation leads us to build in
patterns and routines for appreciation.

Appreciation – Vision
From appreciation we can return to our vision,
and see how it is supported to come into reality.

Connected contentment – Vari Gleeson, lutruwita/Tasmania,[1] Australia

While co-designing with a friend I became intrigued by an emotional response I experienced on arrival at the appreciation anchor point.

After some reflection, on my next personal design I decided to begin with appreciation and explore connections between this and other anchor points.

I started with two generic appreciation notes: one for myself taking the time and effort and one for the Design Web.

Then a third related directly to the new topic. A few months previously, I sold my house and quit my job, enabling me to pursue creative work, study to gain new skills, and contribute to co-emerging regenerative culture. I currently live in a caravan with no fixed address. I felt appreciation for having this opportunity.

Beginning this way, I felt grounded and focused before visiting the rest of the anchor points.

I wanted this design to help make the most of my opportunity, to nurture whatever brings me into a satisfying, supportive and productive life.

Developing my **vision**, I named it Connected Contentment, then worked through it in a clockwise manner. On reaching appreciation I revisited each of the others, looking through the lens of appreciation. This approach worked well for me, bringing into view much more for me to write under appreciation than I had managed in previous designs, enhancing what I had for the anchor points and sometimes surfacing a new viewpoint. Something obvious for me to appreciate is having enough money to live while I create, study and see what happens. Looking at **limits** through the lens of appreciation, I found I am grateful that I don't have enough money to buy my own property, as there are now opportunities for creativity, connection and innovation that otherwise I wouldn't have explored.

This design follows on from one I made for my personal culture. I embroidered a representation onto my jacket: a triskele – a triple spiral. In it I read Mindfulness and Awareness, Journalling and Gratitude, Pause and Reflection. The three spiralling arms work for this design too. I read them as Security, Authenticity, Connection.

In taking an appreciation focused approach, I felt more connected to the design, and more positive and open during the process. I liked how it flowed. It has become a living, functioning part of my life. I can feel it like a web within and around me.

In the co-design mentioned earlier, my friend and I both expressed appreciation for having the other to collaborate with. Making this point explicit has strengthened our connection and commitment to the design, the process and each other.

For the future, I'm looking forward to collaborative designing with a focus on appreciation, to see what happens.

1 lutruwita is the palawa kani (palawa language) name for Tasmania

REFLECTION

Places to visit

Reflection invites us to honestly take stock of the situation. We rarely start with a blank canvas, more often than not there has been activity in the area. There is the old joke of someone asking for directions and the reply being, 'Well I wouldn't start from here'. But of course we are starting from where we are, so visiting reflection early on is beneficial for us to really understand where we are now, in order to know how to get to where we want to.

Later on with the journey it is important to revisit reflection frequently to check whether we are moving forwards or having challenges. From these reflections we are then often directed back to one of the other anchor points.

There could be new emergent things that are arising, unexpected yields that could be glanced over and not given the attention needed if we don't reflect. These emergent properties can at times lead us off in delightful directions and add whole new dimensions to our **vision.**

There are other times when reflection reveals that we are really not making as much progress as we expected. This is time to review **limits**, **action** and others. Was our **action** plan unrealistic, are there **limits** that we didn't account for? Have we fallen back into unhelpful **patterns**? Are there some **helps** which we are not yet using?

As with **appreciation**, reflection also includes sharing when, with whom and how you are going to add regular reflection times and cultivate healthy habits.

We are looking both inwards and outwards. Reflecting on ourselves, how we feel, how we have grown, what we have learnt about ourselves, and looking outwards to see what has changed around us, what has shifted in our relationships, what are the cultural contexts we are existing within?

With reflection we are evaluating the manifestation. Are we on track? What are the yields and benefits that we are gaining? MAKE PROGRESS VISIBLE reminds us to be explicit and celebrate these yields. It is empowering and motivating to see how far we have come on our journey.

Tools and methods for exploring

- Tracking statistics and numbers
- Surveys and questionnaires
- Evaluation forms
- Storytelling
- Testimonials
- Opening a time capsule

- Feedback sessions
- PMI – Positives, Minuses, Interesting
- SWOC – Strengths, Weaknesses, Opportunities, Constraints
- Quiet time
- Journalling
- Historical records
- Roses, thorns, seeds: the beautiful things, the spiky challenging things, and the lessons to take forward

Wisdom from the more-than-human world

Be like a dragonfly with 360° vision

The dragonfly has nearly 360 degrees vision. Each eye has up to 30,000 lenses which function separately, gathering and sharing information with the brain to quickly adjust their flight path. They have multidirectional flight, and an exceptional ability to change direction in mid flight. Dragonflies can fly backwards effortlessly with the same strength as forwards. While less well known than the butterfly for its emergence, it is nonetheless miraculous how it emerges and transforms from being an underwater larva into the beautiful fast flying creatures. As dragonflies zip across the pond, they are reflected in the water.

Embodiment

The movement that embodies reflection is walking forwards, while looking over your shoulder every now and again to see your footsteps. The qualities we inhabit are honesty and thoughtfulness.

Avoid

When receiving feedback it is easy to take things personally, if people tell us how things didn't work well for them. We might get defensive about it and try and explain how things turned out that way. It is a practice to try and avoid taking things personally, to just receive the feedback and extract the information that helps you find lessons to take forward.

Blame and guilt often go hand in hand with reflection. Blame and guilt have the same underlying thought, that someone did something wrong. Blame is directed at someone else's faults, guilt is pointing the finger back at ourselves. But there is always a unique set of circumstances and contributing factors that are intertwined to bring about the results, and we cannot find the exact cause of any mistakes or delays or getting lost. The important thing is to harvest the lessons learnt from the experience to take forward.

Cultural awareness

Mainstream culture has most of its attention on looking forward, reaching for the next thing rather than taking time to learn from the past. There is a tendency to shy away from feedback. It perhaps reminds us of school, or unkind ways that it has been done in the past. It can give a sense of being wrong, or not enough.

Liberate and discover

In a sense whenever we reflect we also have a chance of a new beginning. We start afresh with a recalibration of where we currently are. It is like the fine tuning of our navigation system, with the ability to course correct as needed.

Every adventure is special, every day is unique, every day in a garden or a relationship is different. With reflection we are able to appreciate these differences and the opportunity to start each day afresh with new insights and lessons brought forward.

The art of asking thoughtful questions is the essence of unlocking the wisdom of this anchor point. With the right framing and open-ended questions we invite deeper wisdom to flow through.

Weave and dance

Reflection – Patterns
From our reflections we can move from the details to the underlying patterns of thinking, behaving and interacting.

Reflection – Ideas
As we reflect, ideas will come forth about ways of doing things differently in the future.

Reflection – Appreciation
Part of our reflection will be appreciating what has gone well, and the support that we have received and the benefits gained.

Taming the side quest – Emma Gorbutt, UK

The Side Quest is a wild horse turning this way and that, following its interest, curiosity and running where and when it wants on its own unique terms. Take this energy, put it in a brain and ask it to do a series of set and dull tasks and you have a recipe for unfinished projects, missed deadlines and random chaos... or so many would have us believe. But this doesn't need to be the case.

When I first learned how to use the Design Web and visited reflection, I had an epiphany, I am at the centre of every design. I had previously created many projects but had always viewed myself as something other, and unrelated to the success or failure of what I was creating. When actually if I don't properly integrate all my best bits, and manage or improve my less than helpful patterns, then I won't be making the most effective design.

The 'side quest' phrase is a way of describing how some neurodiverse brains rapidly move from one task to another and another. I am dyslexic and I find multiple paths to solve a problem. Finally I had the term side quest to describe my wild and free brain. Some brains seek a dopamine hit each time a new thing is experienced. For me it is like a dance from one to the next to the next to the next in turn. Which means jobs get done but take longer than they would if I had completed one task at a time.

When I visit reflection, I start by looking back at all the other anchor points. **Ideas** and **helps** will be brimming with potential and ways to overcome the **limits**. But **momentum** is only full of 'good intentions'. Across multiple designs in reflection I have seen ingrained **patterns**. My design Taming the Side Quest came from the combination of **integration** and reflection across multiple designs, how I start so well but can't quite WORK TO COMPLETION; this led to the needs of maintaining steady focus and utilising my strengths.

I spent a lot of time in reflection, following each thread or idea to tame the wild horse. One huge reflection was that I, and society, think these side quests are negative. I reframed them, and thought of them as an immense gift of creativity, resourcefulness and problem solving. They just need careful tending and honouring to be useful. An uncontained fire is dangerous, a well tended fire brings warmth, connection, healing and dinner. So now I have been supporting myself, with reflection, to make good choices when a side quest presents itself. Is this where I intended to be? Is this procrastination, distraction or an immediate reward based action? STOP... Or is this helping right now? Is this seeding something for the future? Is this observing and taking advantage of a new opportunity? Great, go for it. If it feels right I appreciate all the creative emergence it may lead to.

PAUSE

Places to visit

The pause anchor point is about weaving fun, relaxation, creativity and joy into our design adventures. Pause invites us to step away from the intensely focused, driven way of life. We are still productive but in a more relaxed flow state.

There are four approaches to pause.

The first is to take a pause from our design and our actions towards our visions, to step away and take a nourishing break.

The second way is thinking about how we can bring pause into our design methodology. Designing in nature, using artwork, and while having a meal together all bring nourishment into the process.

The third way is using pause as a way of contributing to meeting the needs identified in **integration**. For example, if we want to learn something, what are the nourishing ways in which we can learn? Do we find learning from books, films or with others fun? How can we bring more fun into what we are doing, such as putting music on while we clean, or having a meeting outside?

The fourth way is to identify needs from pause to incorporate into our list of needs in **integration**, such as relaxation, having fun, creativity.

The purpose of pause is to increase calm and connection, to rejuvenate ourselves and each other, to replenish our energy. Weaving intentional pauses throughout our day nourishes us deeply. With pause we LEAVE SPACE FOR EMERGENCE.

Tools and methods for exploring

- Nature connection
- Artwork
- Music, dancing, song
- Poetry
- Daydreaming
- Following your joy
- Reading
- Take a question for a walk and talk, with a friend or collaborator.

Wisdom from the more-than-human world

Be like a cat and take a nap

My cat Milky started my journey of finding more-than-human beings for each of the anchor points. She would come and sit with me whenever I was in the relaxed state of drawing while making the CEED deck. I also enjoyed the pun of pause and paws.

Cats will take any opportunity to have a nap: they have many sleeping places. Cats are also ready to play. Cats are fully present with whatever they are doing. Milky is happy to be at her sit spot on top of a fence post intently watching the world go by. I imagine her to be in a deeply philosophical mood, although she might just be waiting for some prey.

Embodiment

Take a seat, or have a lie down in the hammock or on the ground looking up at the trees. With pause we are feeling calm and restful. We might also feel energised and fully alive and activated. Whether energised or calm, there is a sense of enjoyment that permeates our mind and body.

Avoid

This is time to leave the job lists behind. Let go of 'shoulds'. Leave the guilt behind; pausing while feeling guilty for pausing is counterproductive. Let go of the need to hurry and rush. Avoid faffing and procrastinating about your pause activities; this easily erodes your pause time.

Cultural awareness

We live in a 24/7 world where there are increasing expectations for us to be on call at all times. We inherit work ethics from our parents, our schools and education and from our workplaces themselves. Typically a pause comes when we are ill, as being ill is an acceptable reason for missing school or work, but it doesn't seem as acceptable to pause to rejuvenate and prevent us from becoming ill. Often we are only allowed, by ourselves and others, to pause when we are too exhausted to do anything else.

Even while being a parent there are implicit and explicit messages that self-care is selfish, or at least not a priority, something to do when everyone else is cared for and everything else is done.

We are constantly told not to waste time, and to find ways of saving time – but not so that we can spend it doing the things that we enjoy, but so that we can do more work. There is a separation between work and play. And a sense that work is something that we must do to earn money, but not something to do with joy and purpose and fulfilment.

Liberate and discover

Regularly visiting pause, we recognise pause as a way of being. We can refer to it as pausing, with more awareness of the different ways that could be and how that feels to us.

With pause we regulate our nervous system, we activate the parasympathetic nervous system, associated with relaxation. We come into alignment with our energy levels, with our bliss, with our passions and interests. Pause activities activate different brainwaves which then open up different perspectives and ideas. With pause we come into the present and the principle PRESENCE IN THE PROCESS.

With pause we access a flow state, where pathways open up to us. We value pause and want to visit it often.

Weave and dance

Pause – Ideas
Having fun and play leads to more creative ideas.
Through pausing our imagination has time to activate.

Pause – Momentum
There is a relationship between pause and momentum.
It is often thought that pausing will lead to a loss of momentum,
but pausing can actually give us more momentum.

Pause – Appreciation
As we take time to relax, maybe stepping outside into nature,
we open up to the awe and wonder. We step into appreciation.

Cause for pause – Georgia Brooker, Scotland

Pause has felt especially significant for me in recent designs and in my life. To begin with, in my early efforts, I followed the visual order of the Design Web as though it was a clock, arriving at pause last in the process, generally feeling depleted and in desperate need of rest. I've noticed, however, that my pattern in the past has often been to keep going and going until I hit exhaustion, at which point I have little choice or control of my need to pause, as it hits me like a brick and I feel physically incapable of doing anything but stopping for rest.

While the end of a project can be a very valid place to stop and recoup, what I've realised with further designs is that pause has enormous and essential value as a muster point throughout the process: a calm, quiet starting place to meditate and gather energy for a challenging project at any point in the journey. In more recent designs I have experimented with placing it differently: at the very beginning as a reflective space to refuel my enthusiasm and to gather my thoughts, or in the middle as a place to review progress and change tack where needed. It's become a natural point, or series of points, where I can recalibrate and make best use of my energy.

Reflecting on my microgreen design for a Greener Mind – in which my aim was to develop simple, playful, creative practices that boost everyday well being for myself and my family, and help to build my confidence in creativity for future design work – the whole thing seems saturated with small, sustaining pauses. Part of the essential rhythm of everyday life with my young and energetic kids has now become to build in micro-opportunities to pause and gather my energy within busy days. For me that can be stepping outside and consciously noticing something joyful; creating a beautiful outdoor sit spot to feel connected to the natural world; prioritising a few minutes daily to focus on my breath, to meditate, or practise qigong, or to sing, and to allow creativity to then flow from that spaciousness, often in the form of drawing or creative writing. It's not for nothing that people talk about a 'pregnant pause': pause is the still, fertile emptiness of the feminine Yin principle from which life and action grows.

Becoming more aware of the process of pausing has helped to give me the mental space to respond more often, rather than react, to challenging circumstances, and has supported a renewal of my sense of appreciation, creativity and joy. Pause is sustaining, restorative, and vital.

Part 4

Exercising our designer's mind

The Design Web is a framework that holds the whole design. Within that, as we have seen in the previous part, there are many tools available, as ways to explore the different anchor points. These tools are used to clarify our thinking and take us deeper; some are particularly suited to one or two anchor points, others are more universal and adaptable to any of them. You could use tools from many different places. People translate tools from behavioural science, engineering, teaching, occupational therapy, horticulture, coaching, meditation and many more places. You are welcome to play and explore and adapt any thinking, reflection, teaching and therapeutic tools that you know of. Within my other books I have shared many more tools for personal growth and effective group work. The tools that I explore here are from the Cultural Emergence toolkit. These tools are woven together with the Design Web to become an integrated whole.

In this part, I show how the phases of Cultural Emergence evolve and flow over the life of the design. I explore how to use nature connection, creative expression and embodiment. I take a deep dive into using the seven ways to think differently to reflect and vision. We then look at the other practices of Cultural Emergence that exercise our designer's mind. An additional benefit is to bring these practices alive as an integrated part of your personal and group culture.

Cultural Emergence phases

There are three phases of Cultural Emergence – CHALLENGE AND AWAKEN; MOVE AND INVIGORATE; NOURISH AND EMPOWER.

> CHALLENGE AND AWAKEN is when we loosen the status quo and explore possibilities. We believe change is possible and needed, even if we don't know how or what as yet.
>
> MOVE AND INVIGORATE is centred on the desire to find ways to contribute and have positive impacts in the world. We create pathways forward for our lives and projects.
>
> NOURISH AND EMPOWER is the time to connect with ourselves, each other and the more-than-human world. We rejuvenate ourselves with fun, creativity and self-care.

Change is most effective when we have all three phases in balance. This balance will be different for each of us, and will vary according to the day, week, season, time of our life and other variables. The balance is dynamic and through observation we know when and how to adapt.

Our adventures will be contributing to one or more of the phases, and this might shift over the course of the design. There might be an initial CHALLENGE AND AWAKEN as we begin and our attention goes to the problem. When there is some momentum and we are beginning to implement it, the MOVE AND INVIGORATE phase is enlivened. Design methods that NOURISH AND EMPOWER us will support our continued engagement and bring us benefits in and of themselves. **Pause** and **appreciation** particularly bring in the NOURISH AND EMPOWER phase.

The Cultural Emergence toolkit has a set of practices that stimulate each of these phases. These practices can be used independently throughout our daily lives as well as used as tools within particular anchor points or woven into the overall process. They support us to widen our thinking and feeling, let go of cultural conditioning, embrace change and look for possibilities. Each of the phases activates different aspects of our designer's mind and resources our inner designer with different skills, abilities and ways of seeing the world.

Make connection first

Connection practices are a keystone routine for the NOURISH AND EMPOWER phase. They support us to connect deeply with ourselves, others and the more-than-human world. Jon Young has specialised in connection practices for decades and his experience and wisdom has helped me to bring even more nature connection into my design adventures.

Sit area and timeless wandering

There are two nature connection practices which Jon Young describes. The sit spot or sit area is a place you visit regularly, ideally at least once a day. Literally having it right on your doorstep helps you to visit it frequently. It is a place to come and observe and be, and allow your nervous system to settle. After 20 minutes the beings that went quiet as you arrived will sense that you are not a threat and resume their activities; the birds will start to sing again. Over time the other beings that live there will get used to you and go about their life without stopping when you arrive.

Go to your sit spot frequently and indeed go outside as often as possible. Why be inside when you can be outside? Make it a habit to find activities that can be taken outside, such as eating, phone calls, reading, taking a nap, designing.

Timeless wandering is another practice, where you go for a wander without a schedule or destination. Instead of your rational mind planning the route, you allow your intuitive body wisdom and nature to guide you. Tune into where your body wants to go, and also look at the landscape and see what clues there are that draw you in.

Both of these activities work wonders for our designer's mind. Taking questions into nature and either having a sit spot or a timeless wander will invariably give us answers and inspiration that we would not have found otherwise.

Using nature connection with different anchor points

The roots of permaculture are within observation of nature. Learning how nature operates to create life enhancing, no waste, sustainable systems was the inspiration for creating no waste, life enhancing, productive food producing systems. The **principles** observed in nature inform our designs.

The more-than-human world existed billions of years before our species came into being. Our modern human selves are just a blink of an eye of Earth's history. There are 4.5 billion years of evolution, emergence, research and development. Earth has been on a giant design adventure, discovering the most effective life strategies for millions of species. Weaving together complex self-maintaining interconnected ecosystems. Ecosystems are multilayered with many things happening all at once, including below the surface. They give us guidance for the **integration** anchor point of how to weave our thoughts together, how to create flows and connections between systems.

Nature is where to go for solace, relaxation, inspiration, guidance, grounding, perspective, support. The more that we weave nature into our designs, the more we weave our relationship to nature, the more we come into relationship with our own nature. Nature connection connects us to the bigger vision, reminding us that ultimately, all of our designs are increasing our capacity to live in harmony with each other and the planet, they are all about growing the ethics of Earth care, people care and fair shares in some shape or form. Our personal visions are nested within these bigger visions for life on Earth. There are ancient practices from all around the world with variations of going into nature to open yourself to listening to the universe and finding or receiving a **vision**.

Being in nature is a way of bringing in **pause**. A place to relax and connect. A way of engaging our subconscious, and allowing the weaving of the design that is happening under our conscious awareness to surface. Obviously nature connects us to the more-than-human world, feeding our sense of belonging on Earth. It also supports our connection to ourselves, to the patterns within our veins, to our hopes and dreams, to our past and future, to our ancestors and ancient kin, to our emotions and thoughts. When we involve others in nature connection we WEAVE UNITY within the group. Being in nature opens our capacity for awe and wonder, it extends our **appreciation** muscles.

Nature gives us direct observation of emergence in action. The world we see is a result of emergence. Emergence is all around us, so much so that we take it for granted. But when we really take time to appreciate the minute details and the big interconnected web of life, it is astonishing. Seeds in relationship with soil and water break out of their shell and start growing. What or who do we need to be in relationship with to start growing? Flowers when pollinated become juicy fruit and food for other beings. Who can benefit from the fruit of our labours? Who can we feed with our fruit? Death becomes compost and fertility and feeds new life. What do we need to complete? What do we need to let go of?

Metaphors come from our observation of nature. What do we see in the landscape that speaks to us about our designs? Such as the spider weaving its web, what is it hoping to catch? What are you hoping to catch with your Design Web? On a misty morning the gorse bushes are covered in spiders' webs crystallised in dew drops. What does that tell me about the design ecosystem that I am trying to create?

Nature is a complex matrix of interconnected patterns. There are annual, seasonal and daily patterns. Moon cycles and tides, water and air flows. For all that we observe there are a multitude of contributing factors. The principle SYNCHRONISE WITH NATURAL PATTERNS AND CYCLES informs our **patterns** anchor point.

Nature reminds us of non-linear growth. Plants and animals grow at different rates; if you were to look at the difference between sunflowers and the oak saplings that the jays planted here at Applewood, you would think that the sunflowers are easily ahead. But the oak will take its time and be there for hundreds of years. We are surrounded by quantum leaps and developmental shifts: when the tadpole becomes the frog, the dragonfly nymph emerges from under water, the seed cracks open, the flower turns to fruit. What are the **helps** needed to grow your **vision**?

Designing in nature is a great **ideas** generator. Use your imagination to gain different perspectives, imagining from the perspective of a tree, insect, bird, mycelium.

Nature is full of action at all times. There is both rhyme and reason to these actions. We can learn from gardening as well as from the wild. As a gardener we are attentive to timing, when we need to sow, weed, water and harvest. This teaches us about sequencing and dependencies for the **action** anchor point, and the principle BE ATTENTIVE TO TIMING.

Nature is the soundtrack to every adventure. How much we attend to this is up to us. It could be just white noise in the background, or it could be an informative, beautiful soundscape full of rich information and melodies. As I write at my sit spot, I hear the high-pitched whistle of red kites, it is a familiar sound so I am not so surprised, but then I realise that it is much more insistent than usual, and with no kite soaring in the air. I turn my attention fully to the sound, and I realise it is coming from one place only on the ridge across the valley, and it must be red kite chicks in their nest calling. Over subsequent days I hear them continuously, until one day I notice that the sound has moved and they have fledged. As a metaphor I think about the timing and needs of projects about to fledge. Birds will send early warning alarm calls when predators are approaching. What are the early warning signals we are getting?

Nature connects us both with the present moment and with larger timescales. The connection works in many directions, inwards and outwards. Through connecting with the more-than-human world, we find a deeper connection with ourselves. We activate our ancient blueprint, the one where we were interwoven with the web of life, aware of all the plants, trees, birds, rocks, insects around us. We connect ourselves with our ancient nervous system that we share with other animals, and all the greater sensory awareness that this gives.

Elemental wisdom

Each of the elements gives us metaphors:

- Fire – teaches us about how to keep fires going, how we build a project from the first spark, feeding the flames with kindling until it is ready for some bigger wood. Recognising the attention needed to tend the fire. All of these are valuable lessons for **momentum**.

- Water – teaches us about **limits**. Water will find a way to flow within or around any limits. Water also teaches us about the **reflection** anchor point. Looking into water at times we see ourselves; at other times we see deep below the surface.
- Air – is invisible and yet connects all of life. There is an in-breath and out-breath rhythm. Air makes its presence known through gentle breezes or huge gusts. We see the effects on the trees and feel it in our hair and hear the sound of it, even when we don't see it directly. In the same way our culture is all around us and influences all of our thinking, feeling, being and doing. Use air as a metaphor for patterns, to explore the unseen **patterns** of thinking that are influencing us. Air could also be thought of in relation to **vision**, and using our imagination to see the invisible.
- Earth – is soil, rocks, sand, strength and growth. It is full of life that supports more life. It is the place of interactions and exchanges. We could use this as metaphors within **helps** and **appreciation**. It is a place of manifestation. Earth could be a metaphor for the whole of the design process. The interaction of all the parts is what leads to manifestation.

8 Shields model

Jon Young has created the 8 Shields model, which takes us through natural cycles. The same pattern of the day is seen in the pattern of the year and our life stages. We can replicate this pattern to create flow and move with natural inclinations. The model also relates to our overall design cycle. Each time of day resonates with an attribute of connection, and this can come alive in us.

Time of day – attribute of connection – role in design cycle

Sunrise – happiness – step into the new beginning

Early morning – vitality – bring in childlike curiosity

Midday – deep listening – listen from growth and solutions emerging

Early afternoon – empathy – seek wisdom from nature

Sunset – truly helpful – recalibrate personal and cultural narratives and identify characters and themes

Twilight – fully alive – observe flow of emotions

Midnight – compassion – sense interconnections and weave unity

Pre-dawn – quiet mind – invite liminal creativity

Move the tools

Creativity is expressed in all manner of ways. This isn't just for people that identify themselves as artists, it is for every one of us. Getting out the paper and coloured pencils or paints is a liberating experience. We shift from our heads and our intellect and access a different part of our inner designer. For those that have had woundings as a child about our ability to create, it may take some repatterning of our inner dialogue to even allow us to start to play. Let go of judgements of what is appearing and whether you are happy with it or not. The process is the yield, not necessarily the end product. If this is the first time in decades that you have done any artwork then it is a big achievement in itself, regardless of what it looks like.

The process is a chance to literally see what is below the surface by bringing it into some external form. This could be a drawing, painting, collage, embroidery, sculpture, land art or photograph. It could also be something that isn't visual, such as a poem, song, dance or music piece.

Having fun and being playful allows for freedom of thought and connection with our inner child. We are using both sides of our brain in the process, encouraging us to see connections and bring together our intuitive and rational aspects. There is emergence between these two aspects of ourselves. A drawing expresses the holistic nature and non-linearity, in a way that words cannot.

We may be lucky enough to create some beauty, but the real goal is to make something that is meaningful to you. What we create may be symbolic or realistic. It is our own interpretation through the process that creates a channel of connection and insight with ourselves; our wisdom, stories and feelings.

For some designs, such as land based ones, or if we were reorganising our living room, then a realistic model or drawing is valuable. We can bring play and effectiveness into the process using card cutouts of the individual elements, such as plants or furniture, and move them around on a base map.

The fundamental principle for any creativity is MOVE THE TOOLS. Show up and see what emerges; when we are actually using our hands, using the paints, cutting things out – then something will happen. Just thinking about it isn't what is needed here. It is by starting that we create pathways for the imagination to meet the material world.

This creativity can be brought into any and all of the anchor points. Even when we are using words we can doodle around the edges, use coloured pencils to highlight something that is particularly important, arrange words in patterns, create icons, draw the symbols and beings for each anchor point.

Here are some ideas for specific anchor points:

Vision – Create a vision or mood board, a collage expressing the qualities of where you would like to get to.

Helps – Draw stick figures of yourself doing different things, to show your skills and experiences.

Limits – Show what the limits are and then how to break through them. Map the limits showing visually how big or small they are. Place them on a bucket so you can see which ones are your base limits. Express the limits in colours and textures.

Patterns – Go into nature and draw a pattern that resonates with you.

Ideas – Invite people to use crayons and paints to free up their imagination.

Principles – Use the Cultural Emergence colouring book[1] to create posters.

Integration – It is incredibly useful to create something visual that represents your design, that you can then keep somewhere in sight and mind. This becomes a portal for you to access all of your thinking.

Action – Making your action plan beautiful helps it to be something that you want to look at and engage with. Draw a river of actions.

Momentum – Draw seasonal and daily cycles.

Appreciation – Add hearts around each of the things you appreciate. Cut out hearts and give them to people with something that you appreciate about them.

Reflection – Create a storyboard of events leading up to now. Draw a river of life, showing the different streams, waterfalls, rocks, flows, beaches. Use artwork as a way to MAKE PROGRESS VISIBLE.

Pause – Just have fun with colour and no plan.

Move the tools

People have used their creativity in all sorts of ways. And even with representations of the Design Web. A friend has made a bracelet with each of the 12 anchor points as charms. Another group in a community garden repurposed the frame of a trampoline to create a weave with the 12 anchor points around it.

The essential part of creative expression is to show up and just see what happens. Celebrate your unique way of expressing yourself. There are endless possibilities for bringing creative expression in.

1 Get the Cultural Emergence colouring book for free by signing up to our newsletter www.cultural-emergence.com

Your body knows

Our Western education is very focused on the intellect of the brain. We learn in a rational way, and are supposed to make decisions with rational thought. While of course logic and thoughtful planning is useful, it isn't the only way.

Tapping into our body wisdom gives access to a deeper level of information. Our body gives us an honest reading about our feelings and preferences, when we learn to listen to it. Two of the most relevant principles here are YOUR BODY KNOWS and HONOUR THE WISDOM WITHIN.

Movement and embodiment are ways of tapping into your body wisdom. Dancing is a fantastic way of expressing your **vision**. Shaking is a great way of letting go of **patterns**. Walking a timeline allows us to feel an **action** plan and how it will unfold over time.

Think about your **limits** and map them all out on paper. Now take a look at the list, and with each one take a body reading, what is your body telling you about them? For some there is little or no reaction in your body. For others, you might feel a clenching in your jaw, a flutter in your stomach, a shift in your breathing, a yawn, a restlessness in your feet. Whatever subtle shift there is, your body will be giving you some useful information about its importance and where you need to focus your attention.

With the **appreciation** anchor point we move from words to the feelings of appreciation in our bodies. That shift moves us into a heart space where we are able to tap into the intelligence of our heart. The principle USE THE INTELLIGENCE OF CO-OPERATING HEARTS reminds us that when people are interacting from a heart space, they are coming from a space of co-operation rather than competition.

Our body is a barometer for our motivation and connects us with **helps** and **momentum**. When we are motivated our bodies are filled with energy, we shrug off our sluggishness and are ready for action.

When we find **principles** that are resonant within our bodies, they will continue to support us throughout, and when we think of them we feel the support in our bodies, not just our minds.

When you come to **integration**, your body will be an invaluable guide to finding and weaving together solutions. When you experience the sense of cohesion, of flow, of ease and wholeness, you will know you are on the right track.

When engaging with **ideas**, if we bring joy and energy into our bodies there will be a more creative flow. Doing activities that involve both sides of our bodies also engages both sides of our brains and therefore brings us more ideas.

Our bodies hold memories within them. Tapping into where those experiences and stories are stored within our bodies enables us to work with them and release any emotional charges for the **reflection** anchor point. (For traumatic experiences this is best done with the support of a trained therapist.)

Vision arrives in our bodies with an expansiveness. The principle BE IN COURAGE reminds us to reframe nervousness as courage surfacing. When we sense our vision sometimes the tingles may feel like nervousness or overwhelm, but it may just be our courage surfacing to meet our vision with bravery and determination.

Pause is something that happens in our bodies. We move into our parasympathetic nervous system. Varied activities will do this for different people. For extroverts, company with people is rejuvenating, for introverts time alone is needed. The important thing is that we experience it as a pause that relaxes and rejuvenates us.

Continued bodily awareness and embodiment support us on all levels of life. There is a reciprocal relationship, with our design practice enabling more bodily awareness and more bodily awareness encouraging more effective designing.

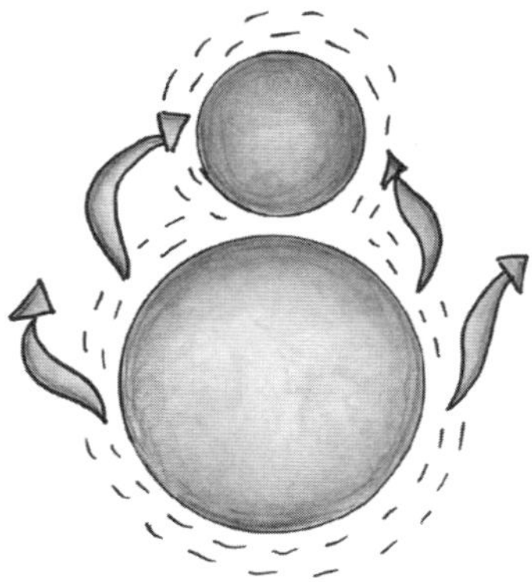

Your body knows

Magic from stillness – Barbara Scheltus, Croatia/the Netherlands

Since I learned to tune into my bodily wisdom, my designs are more 'me', and I finish them easily and with joy.

Designing for me used to be a heady happening; left brain hemisphere logic that I would try to juice up with some creativity later on. That was when I didn't know that I could trust the flow of words that come from a grounded state of being. It was the time that I had no idea about the feelings of joy, excitement or longing in my heart that give me the drive to design and realise my dreams. Or the feelings of openness to life that my gut can produce, that make me integrate and cooperate. And tapping into the stillness in the centre of my head (between the ears, under the crown) my sense of time seems to shift.

I learned to ground myself and sense being held by the Earth. And from that safe space I follow my intuition and then creatively use language and logic to turn my clouds of colourful imaginary experiences into a design.

Grounding myself halts the distracting influx of external opinions and ideas. When I use my imagination to test out ideas, my body wisdom often surprises me with new solutions or **helps**.

The design Growing a Village emerged after tuning into my family and feeling that long-term sharing was missing. It was a quiet voice telling me that the sharing we did wasn't yielding enough. Volunteers and guests are welcomed into the family, they feel at home and our relationship with them builds. And the moment they leave, it is gone. Yes we keep in touch, but the familiarity doesn't come back when people travel further. So out of this realisation the wish for a community of people was born.

With Growing a Village, I tuned into the feeling of having more houses on our terrain. The idea of having more like-hearted families around sits really well with me, but the idea of our building zone overlapping with my garden seemed like a nightmare. How do you move an established garden, balanced soil and systems, already in the ultimate spot? So I imagined beautiful houses, made with natural materials, and then my imagination just positioned them in various spots inside my garden and food forest where they would fit well. Not destroying what is there, but houses harmoniously besides the kale and kiwi, and living in a beautiful, colourful edible landscape for a natural lifestyle. Thank you body wisdom for this solution.

With embodiment I learned to stop pushing and start with a gentle pull on a string of my vision and intentions. I trickle down my sense of being from up in my head to down in my pelvis. From the safe stillness there, the magic happens. I drop a question into the pond and listen. When it hits my passion, the answer is usually a jump of my heart or something else that is loud and enthusiastic. And sometimes I need to find the quiet voices inside and listen really well.

I used to finish a design with gritted teeth and willpower. Now I've learnt willingness instead, and a natural flow that emerges from drive and vision deep within me.

Seven ways to thinking differently in our designs

The paradigms that we live in give us parameters for our dreams, our interactions, our effectiveness, our collaborations. From birth we are culturally conditioned. To step more fully into ourselves it is necessary to let go of many of the mainstream mindsets, and replace them with positive thinking patterns.

One of my standard replies to the FAQ 'What is permaculture?' is that it is a shift in thinking. When we shift our thinking, our activities, projects and outlook on life also change. With my book, *7 Ways to Think Differently*, I sought to examine and unfurl this answer, categorise these shifts and reveal how these new ways differ from mainstream paradigms. The 'seven ways' shared below have come from a distillation of the shifts that occur with permaculture training and practice. The seven ways of thinking can be used as tools for both reflection and visioning, helping us see the cultural paradigms which we might be operating from and encouraging us to move towards more regenerative thinking. For each of the 'seven ways' below I share some of the insights that have come from using them in three of my designs:

- Revitalise Myself, to help my recuperation after months in bed with a broken leg;
- Spring cleaning design that I did with my partner, Chris Evans;
- Creating the CEED deck (Cultural Emergence Empowerment & Design).

The first two bring more vitality into our bodies and homes and are relevant to most of us. The third one is for a bigger creative project that can be adapted to any larger project you are doing or want to do.

I used the 'seven ways' to reflect upon any hidden messages or negative behaviours that might be limiting me, as well as for finding new, more supportive ways of thinking.

Abundance thinking

Be prolific with the seeds you sow for an abundant future

Abundance thinking is an antidote to the pervasive 'not enough' messages surrounding us in all types of guises. For Revitalise Myself, I found that I had a lot of messages that were holding me in a scarcity mindset, such as 'I don't have enough energy', 'I haven't had enough sleep', 'I don't have enough time'. Once I became aware of these, it was easier to catch, question and reframe them to 'abundance thoughts' like 'there is limitless energy in the world to tap into', 'I have all the energy I need'.

With spring cleaning, we asked ourselves 'what do we really need and can we generously find new homes for our surplus?' While creating the CEED deck, I needed to be proactive in reframing my inner narrative about not having enough art skills, and appreciate my willingness to learn and practice. Focusing on internal and external messages and finding gratitude for what I have helps me shift into abundance thinking.

Solutions thinking

See the path not the mountains

With Revitalise Myself, I identified a pattern of ruminating on problems at night and then not sleeping well, which of course affected energy levels. Instead I learnt to consciously bring my attention to solutions. With the spring cleaning design, we thought about how to turn waste into resources. We also sought to go deeper to root causes of clutter to create longer-lasting solutions.

Seeing the path not the mountains was my mantra while creating the 96-card deck. Together with the principle PRESENCE IN THE PROCESS, I was guided to stay focused on whatever I was working on at the time, and just take it one step at a time, rather than getting overwhelmed by thinking of the whole project.

Systems thinking

Dance with life and co-create beautiful murmurations

Engaging with systems thinking for Revitalise Myself, I realised that my ideas about my energy and vitality were quite linear in terms of cause and effect; X amount of sleep = Y amount of energy. I recognised that there were more complex interactions and contributing factors, and that my energy can shift dramatically and non-linearly within moments; particular activities, news, encounters or invitations from friends can lead to disproportionate spikes or troughs of energy. This also illustrated the abundance of energy that is available at any time when the channel is open. When creating our action plan for our spring clean we used systems thinking to decide whether to work on categories, themes, locations, tasks, e.g. shall we sort out all the books, work on one room at a time or spend time fixing things? With the CEED deck I was proactively seeking the emergence and quantum shifts between drafts of creative projects, where new clarity, patterns and cohesion emerge.

Co-operative thinking

The essence of this way is the shift from 'I can't' to 'we can'. For Revitalise Myself, I thought about others around me and how to spend more time with people that bring me energy. Our spring cleaning design became a combined endeavour that helped to make it more fun, effective and peacemaking.

While creating the CEED deck I did a crowdfunder campaign that brought together a community. These people were pivotal not just with raising the money to finance the printing, but contributed significantly with motivation, accountability, encouragement and enthusiasm.

Connect and collaborate with others in the hive

Thinking like nature

Your neurons are shaped like trees. You are nature.

With Revitalise Myself, I realised that I was using artificial energy, such as electric lights, to override or divert my natural inclinations to sleep in the evenings or hibernate in winter. Thinking like nature involves coming into alignment with my own daily, weekly and seasonal flows of energy. Similarly, spring cleaning uses the spring energy and the natural inclinations to cleanse after winter. We also thought more about the process in a cyclical way rather than a linear path to a destination.

I did a lot of the artwork for the CEED deck outside with nature's patterns as inspiration. I was inspired by the many beings at Applewood to create new images for the Design Web. While watching bees on borage plants, I noticed how they only went to the open flowers and thought how that is a perfect representation of the principle BE ATTENTIVE TO SHIFTS, OPENINGS AND OPPORTUNITIES.

Thinking for the future

Spring cleaning was a way of getting ahead of ourselves for the course season at Applewood Permaculture Centre. We realised that every time we do filing or put something away, we are being kind to our future selves. We aim to set up long-lasting solutions that will take less input to maintain in the future. Revitalising Myself was an ongoing process of supporting my recovery, doing my physiotherapy and expanding my comfort zones.

When creating the CEED deck, I kept in mind all the thousands of people around the world who would benefit from interacting with this toolkit, and how future generations of all life on Earth so desperately need the present generation to radically shift towards regenerative cultures. I humbly felt that I was sharing something that could play a small part in supporting others to be part of this tidal change.

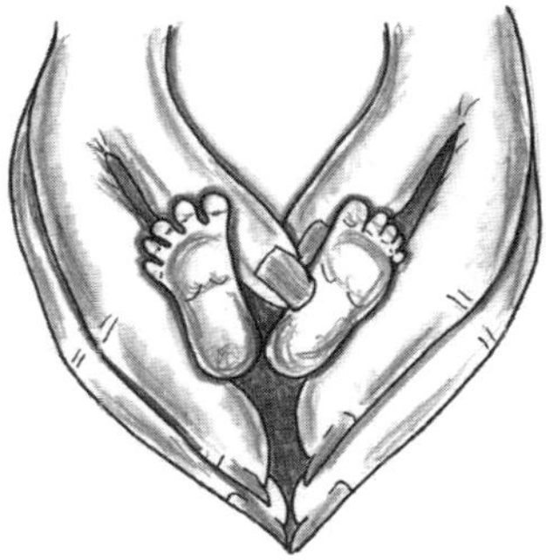

Care and plan for future generations of all species

From thinking to doing

Leapfrog into action

It is not enough to just be thinking about change or to change our thinking, we also need effective action. The principle MOVE THE TOOLS supports this shift into doing. The tools will differ for each job. For creating the CEED deck, the tools were my coloured pencils, with the guidance of show up and see what emerges and create pathways for the imagination to meet the material world.

For spring cleaning, the tools are the hoover, mop and bucket. For creating vitality, a friend shared an idea of using energy to gain energy. So when I experience an ebb in my energy instead of having a lie down and nap, I could use the little bit of energy I have for action, such as going for a walk or exercising, playing music or finding another way to open up the energy channels (although I do still also like my naps!).

Tend to your personal culture

The following practices are shared in the context of exercising our designer's mind. When doing these practices regularly they become embodied and woven into our personal culture. All of these practices can continuously be used to become healthy habits. When used with other people they create healthy group cultures.

Asking questions

At the heart of our exploration of each anchor point is questioning. Questions can activate specific phases. Ones that CHALLENGE AND AWAKEN and take us out of usual ways of thinking, such as in **limits**; questions that MOVE AND INVIGORATE and encourage us to be effective in **action**; questions for **pause and appreciation** that open us to the NOURISH AND EMPOWER phase. Find interesting questions that unlock our thinking and lead us to solutions. Be childlike with your curiosity and thirst to learn and discover. Open up doorways in minds and hearts. Ask questions that connect, expand and deepen.

Storytelling and catching

Stories have the capacity to enhance any of the phases. Designs are stories we are creating. Design by design, chapter by chapter, they are telling the story of our lives, there are characters, plot lines and scenes. Who are you sharing your stories with? How are you telling them? Whose stories are you listening to? When we are creating for or with others, catching their stories enables us to authentically contribute with the most relevant information.

Challenge and awaken phase

Awareness of culture

This is the keystone practice for this phase. It is a constant practice. As we saw in the last part, each anchor point has its own cultural patterns and norms. Most designs will be on some level aiming to shift an aspect of culture. This could be our own personal culture, our group culture or wider. Our process will illuminate some of the previously unseen cultural patterns. Each of us is part of many macro and micro cultures that are influencing our decisions. Macro cultures include our country, gender, race, religion, education; micro cultures are smaller ones such as our particular college, local neighbourhood, family, group. We have cultures around our dietary choices, sports teams, music preferences, economic status and many more categories. Each one is slightly different and some more influential than others. Ask yourself and the group questions about culture. What are the cultural expectations, parameters, norms, tolerances, phobias? What are our ethics, values, priorities? What cultures are influencing the design? From our awareness of culture we come to realise that culture is an active dynamic process that we can influence, and this is one of the effective ways we can facilitate cultural shifts.

Sensing systems

Sensing systems is a way of recognising flows, connections and interactions. Wherever we have placed boundaries in our design is a way in which we have created a system. Being observant to the flows might lead us to move those boundaries in or out. Sensing systems is an important practice for **integration** in particular. Observe systems with multiple senses including intuition. Designs are essentially about finding ways to interact and influence systems and create conditions for emergence.

Wise wording

Language reveals underlying values, beliefs, assumptions, oppression and privilege. Sensitivity is needed with the words we use to describe our **vision**, our **limits**, and more. Filling our **action** anchor point with 'shoulds' is demotivating, compared to the phrases 'choose to, want to or can do'.

Levelling privilege

Each person has their own combination of privileges and lacks of privilege. When working with other people, the process either perpetuates existing privileges and oppression, or supports the dismantling of them. With wise and careful facilitation the process supports all voices to be heard, and awareness brought forth about how to empower everyone. With explicit questions, gentle challenges and subtle observations, levels of privilege which are influencing the issue are revealed and rebalanced. Those with more privilege are invited to find ways to be **helps** for others; giving and opening doors for those with less privilege.

Self and collective responsibility

The very act of embarking on the design is taking responsibility. We are proactively being part of the solution and coming into alignment with our visions, choices and actions. Design allows for collective input, responsibility, accountability and care.

Pattern disruption

All change has PATTERN DISRUPTION at its core, shifting from usual ways of thinking, being, doing, interacting and feeling. Design adventures encourage us to let go of auto pilot and cultural conditioning. Obviously, PATTERN DISRUPTION is part of the **patterns** anchor point, and it also supports us in the others, such as disrupting the standard ways we create **action** plans, **reflect**, or **vision**.

Challenging mindsets

Our beliefs and assumptions hold us within certain parameters, limiting our capacities to **vision** and step into a different future. Designing shines a light on our blindspots and invites us to question beliefs and conventions. Ask the questions 'is this true?', 'are there exceptions?', 'what happens if we put that assumption to one side for a moment?' Letting go of limiting beliefs creates space for us to grow. These beliefs are often ones we have inherited from our micro and macro cultures. Be gentle and mindful of timing and other people's feelings when challenging. The Design Web creates a more neutral way of exploring and challenging mindsets, in less of a personal way when working with others.

Naming and reframing

Form, visibility and direction comes from naming our design. It is a potent moment within the whole process. Naming creates new stories, systems, concepts and ideas. The boundaries we place around our topic create a frame. What happens when we shift that frame? There are also frames of culture, timescales, our humanness, our education, religion, and many other things that direct our perspective. Choosing different frames provides new viewpoints. Try reframing problems as solutions, challenges as opportunities, waste as resources.

Move and invigorate phase

Engaging imagination

The willingness to start a design suggests an ability to imagine a different future. It might just be a spark of an idea that we follow that sets off further ideas and pathways to manifestation. The more we exercise our imagination muscles the more possibilities we see. Without imagination designs are soon stale, boring and predictable. Imagination is an essential ingredient of our adventure. Be creative, resourceful and humorous with your ideas. Actively engage the imagination regularly through play, storytelling and daydreaming, to develop this key skill.

Collaboration and co-creation

A design is rarely just for ourselves, they are collaborations in some way. Collaborations with life, with other people, with networks, with different parts of ourselves. New opportunities, insights and possibilities arise from collaborating. By supporting each other and working together we achieve much more. Make a practice to consider who you are collaborating with, and how and what you can co-create together.

Growing in effectiveness

Designing helps us to clarify the effects we are wanting to have in the world. It supports us to utilise our time, energy and resources well in order for our contributions in the world to have the maximum effect. Our capacity and confidence increases over time. Working regularly with microgreen designs supports us to grow in effectiveness.

Building resilience

Permaculture has a strong focus on practical resilience strategies. Practical solutions in our daily lives, homes and gardens that support us to move towards the ethics.

Resilience is also about emotional resilience and the ability to recover from adversity. To allow challenges to transform us, and help us to bounce with, bounce back or bounce forwards. Designing supports us to meet life's challenges in a proactive way. Spreading resilient strategies in our communities may be our explicit intention and is a way of contributing further to Earth care, people care and fair shares.

Nourish and empower phase

Listening

The art of listening allows us to tune into the deeper wisdom of ourselves and other people. Listen for subtle nuances, for what isn't being said, for emotion, for sparks of energy. Listening authentically to someone is a gift that allows them to explore themselves further. Allow others to follow their own thoughts, ideas and feelings. Giving full attention to someone without interruption or judgement will provide rich information. With practice and care we learn to listen to the design itself, as if it was a living being giving its own responses and wisdom.

Building trust

Through successive projects we build trust in our skills, and trust in the Design Web. Trust that pathways will emerge, trust that we can listen and adapt, trust that our imagination is vast and active, trust that small steps will lead to bigger changes, trust that answers will come and pieces will fall into place. Building trust with others, through creating a field of encouragement where everyone feels safe to share their voice, encourages everyone to shine their gifts and skills and effectively collaborate. Moving from microgreen designs to bigger ones allows trust in our inner designer to grow at an organic rate. Trust allows us to relax into emergence. Trust yourself to bring your gifts more fully into the world, finding your purpose and contribution.

Supporting emotions to flow

Designing has the capacity to uncover deeply buried feelings, wounds, grief, concerns, longings and passions. It is a chance to put ourselves back on track, but might involve some grieving as to why we were taken off track in the first place. Emotions are useful signposts on our adventure, we might want to shy away from them, but they are usually pointing us to a place of transformation.

Many of us feel sadness about the state of the world, although we might not connect with this often. Allowing ourselves to fully feel this then releases this energy to fuel our desire, courage and commitment for change.

Allowing for more challenging emotions to flow also allows more joy, bliss and happiness into our designs.

Self-care

Designing for ourselves is an act of self-care. It is a way of prioritising our own needs, supporting ourselves on physical and emotional levels. The essence of **pause** is about weaving self-care throughout. Self-care doesn't necessarily mean being alone; there are ways to join with others to do self-care activities. Nurturing our inner designer means embracing imperfection, allowing for growth and play.

Surfacing gifts

Each of us has a unique set of talents, skills, internal resources and qualities, even though we may not be aware of all of them. The more we design, the more we discover about ourselves. We develop a relationship with our inner designer and surface gifts. With **helps** we are continually invited to voice our gifts, experiences and skills. Eventually we can do this without perceived limiting voices saying we are being arrogant or big headed. The more helpful we are the more gifts we discover in ourselves. Through the **appreciation** anchor point we are invited to see gifts in others and tell them, inviting them to shine. The world needs all of us to shine our genius.

Growing ropes

Each time you connect with a person or more-than-human being you add a strand of connection that thickens and strengthens, in the same way a rope is made of many strands. Use the Design Web to strengthen your ropes of connection with the more-than-human world. Grow ropes to your vision by repeatedly bringing it into awareness and voicing it out loud. Grow ropes to your designs by visiting them regularly. Over time you will grow ropes to each of the anchor points, forming unique relationships that strengthen every time we visit them.

Peacemaking

Designing is an act of peacemaking. We are intentionally making steps to come into alignment. When collaborating with my partner, Chris, we have found it a way of clearing the air and exploring issues without assigning blame. It is a way of integrating parts of ourselves, and making peace with our past.

Peacemaking begins with taking responsibility for our own personal peace, and being familiar with the feelings of peace in our bodies. It then moves to our awareness of the impact of our words and energies on one another. It also extends into the recognition that past, personal, ancestral, and cultural experiences all affect the current situation and design.

Weaving community fire – Leona Johnson, UK

My journey with the Design Web began with a walk in nature, carrying the seed of an idea. I had a desire to run a Questing with Fire programme, where people would build relationships with themselves, with fire and with each other. I let the **vision** guide me, allowing inspiration to flow from the land around me. When I returned, I spread the anchor points on pages across the floor, in front of the fire in my living room, pouring the insights I had gathered into each one. This process helped me see the layers of possibility and structure, grounding a dream into something actionable.

The design's foundation was built anchor point by anchor point. **Vision** was the spark – our dream of an intergenerational community grounded in connection and ceremony.

From there, **helps** illuminated the resources we could draw on: the land, mentors, fellow teachers, the growing interest in rites of passage, my training community and a network of like-minded souls. I wrote these down, noticing how each help supported another. **Patterns** showed me what was already thriving in my life and revealed the structures I could adapt from cultural practices that align with emergence. I had been working with the 8 Shields for six years in our business at that point. I explored these models and patterns by sketching mind maps, finding inspiration in traditional ceremonies for honouring the elements and life stages and gatherings from other cultures. At every stage, **reflection** was a guiding companion, helping me adjust and refine what emerged.

Limits presented themselves early. Time, energy, and the scope of what we wanted to achieve all needed to be acknowledged. I leaned into emergence to find a balance between structure and intuition, trusting that the process would reveal the right steps. Through **integration**, I wove the strands together, ensuring that each element felt aligned with the **vision** and the community's needs. This stage involved repeatedly returning to the anchor points, layering detail upon detail, and ensuring that no aspect was left behind.

Each anchor point plays a crucial role, and I have learned that when flow is interrupted, it often reveals an overlooked aspect of the Design Web. When challenges arose, such as coordinating diverse community needs or adapting to unforeseen logistical issues, the anchor points offered clarity. For example, when tensions surfaced during a group ceremony, we revisited the **reflection** anchor point, pausing to ask what was missing in our approach. This simple act of asking questions opened space for deeper understanding and strengthened our cohesion.

By the time our planning was complete, I felt the programme had a life of its own – a dynamic system that could evolve with the people it served. Facilitating the fifth cohort now, I see how this design continues to offer depth and resilience. People are returning to help support new cohorts and the fire family, as we call them, is growing; growing in numbers, effectiveness and connection. What we have created is an intergenerational, awakened, and inspired community, sustained by the healthy, connected self leadership inherent in the design. Witnessing this community expand in consciousness has been awe-inspiring

– an example of deep healing, regeneration, and hope manifesting in real life. We envisioned a depth of connection and community that has blossomed into an embodied experience of Cultural Emergence. The anchor points remain an invaluable tool, not just in sustaining the programme but in helping me reflect and adapt as we grow.

This process has reaffirmed my gratitude for the Design Web. It's not just a method but a living practice, one that continues to guide me in creating spaces for connection, healing, and cultural regeneration. Each step in the process deepened my own understanding of what it means to weave community and culture with intention.

Part 5

Awakening the collective design spirit

At some point you are likely to want to expand your designing to include other people. This could be family, friends, community groups, work colleagues. There are endless possibilities. It is exciting to feel the potential for making our collaborations and relationships more connective, streamlined, ambitious and effective. Creating with others is living the principle MANY MINDS ARE BETTER THAN ONE. There is a collective design spirit that emerges where there is greater wisdom, enthusiasm and potential.

In this part we explore how to adventure effectively with others, how to set up a design culture, the potential challenges and benefits, facilitation options and cross-cultural considerations. We cover how to use it informally as well as in more formal settings of coaching and teaching the Design Web. We conclude with top tips for collaboration.

Use the intelligence of co-operating hearts

Our design muscles get a good workout when working with other people. There are so many more perspectives, challenges, ideas, dynamics, hidden beliefs. There is an exponential level of complexity as we are all bringing our personal cultures and our inner designers. There are all the interactions and combinations of all of those cultures plus the emergent properties of the group entity. Some of the group culture may have evolved before any of the existing members were even a part of the group. The group has its own internal landscape as well as outer face. The principle EMERGENCE HAPPENS IN RELATIONSHIP emphasises how all of the exchanges and interactions will bring emergence that wouldn't have been possible by ourselves.

As we saw for our own lives, it can be both overwhelming and exciting to see all the potential projects. Either way we need to be strategic about where we give our attention so that it falls on fertile ground and grows rather than withers. The same advice for ourselves applies to others. Choosing small, boundaried designs with quick results helps people to actually feel the benefits and want to do more. The first steps are often just to get agreement to enter into a process, and decide a topic.

One of the key requirements for being able to design with and for others is to have an ongoing practice for yourself. With this you will be able to talk from first hand experience. You will be more able to distinguish when a group is getting tied up due to the complexities of the process, or due to group dynamics surfacing, and hence be able to find a way to navigate through either. Whether with friends, groups, teaching or coaching, sharing your own designs and anecdotes is a potent way of encouraging and enrolling people into trying it for themselves.

Creating your design culture

When stepping into a design with other people, we are entering into a unique space of exploration. Agreeing a culture for this process first helps to build connections. Defining what, who and how you are going to be designing together is important to the flow that follows.

Sometimes it is appropriate to make a quick plan for your design culture. This is an acknowledgement that it is going to be different from your everyday interactions. It helps people to let go of usual patterns of interacting and set intentions for a cohesive adventure.

Vision the qualities you want to bring in. Think about how to bring regular times of **appreciation** and **reflection**. What are the **limits**? What are the needs for the **integration** anchor point, such as scheduling time, creating documents, decision making? What are the existing helpful **patterns** of meetings and working together?

What are the **helps** each person is bringing? And so forth with all of the anchor points. Your design culture gathers time, space and motivation.

This might be too advanced and meta level thinking for those new to it, and so can be done by yourself without the rest of the group, and then the essence shared together. The important thing for the group is to make sure everyone is on board with entering into and co-creating a special safe and creative space and culture. It creates a unique space for exploring together, inviting all voices to be heard. Through this you are being proactive in making the process distinct and inviting different outcomes.

People like to adventure in a variety of ways, and sharing this at the beginning helps to understand each other. Some people will just want to get on and do things, others will want to build relationships before making decisions, others will take time making decisions but then be very committed to following those decisions through, others will want to leave decisions to the very last moment to allow for spontaneity and flexibility. None of these are wrong approaches in themselves, but without acknowledgement they could lead to misunderstandings and conflict.

The process is as important as the destination. Staying connected and growing relationships through the process is as, or even more, important than the final design. Having fun together will make the whole journey smoother.

Myself and my partner, Chris, have done this several times over the years as a way of aligning ourselves, helping us to connect with the benefits as well as move through **limits**. We have found it valuable, but it can be time consuming and feel like a distraction from getting on with the actual design at times. We have found solutions to this by setting a time limit on it, and interweaving designing our culture with working on the current project.

Starting each session with a check-in, appreciation and update on actions is helpful and brings in the principle MAKE CONNECTION FIRST.

Other people are often both the biggest **helps** and **limits**. Taking time to create a supportive and encouraging culture steers people to being **helps** rather than **limits**.

Paying attention to our culture can in itself bring many benefits into our everyday patterns of interacting. Our existing group culture influences our design culture, and this permeates back into our group culture.

Facilitation

One of the things that you can work out in your culture is how to share ownership of it, so that it doesn't just feel like one person wants it to happen. Ownership isn't the same as facilitation, but agreeing the facilitation will bring a sense of co-ownership, whereas if one person just assumes the facilitation role, then it can be perceived that they have more ownership, and others less.

There are different facilitation options, each with their advantages and disadvantages. Having one facilitator has the advantage of them being able to hold the overview and continuity between sessions. The disadvantage is that there can be too much emphasis on their particular style, or that they seem to have more investment than others. Rotating gives more shared ownership and diversity of methods, and can be done by alternating between people, or doing it as a pair. An outside facilitator will be able to be neutral and provide external viewpoints, but won't have as much understanding of the nuances of what is happening.

Having named facilitators helps keep the process on track. Their responsibilities include ensuring everyone has the chance to speak, using different tools, planning questions in advance, keeping discussions relevant and on topic. Other roles, such as timekeeper and note taker, can also be defined and rotated.

It is good to create a flow between times when everyone is working together and times when the group is split into small groups or pairs, and time for solo thinking. Pulsing between these options maintains interest and gives more space for insights and emergence.

As the group becomes more skilled and fluent, a more collaborative self-organising facilitation evolves. Although there are times when this ends up being a case of 'too many cooks spoil the broth' and it is easier when one person takes leadership for a time.

The principle ANYONE CAN RAISE THE VIBRATION reminds the facilitator to release control, and allow for any person in the group to give suggestions to improve the process and bring energy into the group. These could be practical ones, such as opening a window for fresh air, or creative ideas for the process.

However the facilitation happens, the essential things are to support an inclusive, connecting space where people feel safe to give honest reflections. The aim is to create a fertile space for creativity to flourish, while also being grounded and pragmatic leading to achievable actions and movement towards the collective vision.

Challenges of designing with others

Many challenges will appear on your adventure together, but if worked through together these will WEAVE UNITY in the group. Not everyone will immediately welcome stepping into a design adventure. We might be met with resistance, which shows up in various ways: arguments, disengagement or procrastination. Over enthusiasm can also be challenging and lead to scattered energy.

Right from the beginning, when deciding your topic, it will become apparent that people have different priorities. This will continue with differing priorities about what to spend money on, timescales, aesthetics, quality, health and safety and much more. Navigating these is part of what needs to be worked through. When these perspectives are given voice the design supports the group to find the sweet spot of compromise, or even better, the emergence of new ideas and possibilities that are outside of what anyone previously thought of by themselves.

Grudges and past conflicts may surface or be just below the surface influencing or derailing the current conversation. It is often an emotional journey.

Within any group there is a range of privileges and lack of privileges, these might be due to gender, class, age, ethnicity, education. It could be because of experience or time in an organisation. These privileges play out with who needs to compromise, whose ideas are listened to and who gets the final say.

Following through is important. If design doesn't turn into action then it can feel like a waste of time and be counterproductive.

Collaboration often takes a lot more time than just making decisions by yourself. However it gives a more holistic and long-lasting plan that involves everyone.

Benefits of designing with others

Jon Young shares a saying from tracking, "You are always right when tracking alone." When you see a footprint in the sand and you conclude it is a fox and there is no-one to challenge that, your belief is untested, and you proceed as if it is true. With someone else there, they can point out the size or shape or tiny detail that suggests something else. This is the same with designing by ourselves, we fall into our usual parameters, expectations and beliefs. When we have others with us, they help us step out of our comfort zones, assumptions, and cultural contexts.

Other people bring ideas, enthusiasm, skills and experience that enable more progress. They bring new perspectives that support a bigger vision. There is a social scape being gardened. Each person is a different plant, with unique characteristics, growth rates, needs and beauty. The culture supports the feeling of everyone contributing to the whole. A field of encouragement is created where the principles of GIVE ENCOURAGEMENT and RECEIVE ENCOURAGEMENT come alive and everyone is connected to their own heart and supported to shine their gifts, and the group and individuals flourish.

Learning the languages of design and Cultural Emergence enables the group to weave stories and integrate these tools and thinking into all interactions and projects.

Designing together gives shared ownership of projects, which then leads to more motivation and momentum. People feel able to take initiative because they understand the underlying needs and the bigger vision of where everyone is heading for.

Describing the deer – Jon Young, USA

When I started working with Looby and the Design Web it took me a few designs to find my own flow. But once I did I could see exciting possibilities for the projects that I was working on with various teams. With each of the courses that Looby and I co-facilitated, more and more team members joined in until we reached a critical mass of around half the team. It was then easy for us to use Design Web collectively in team meetings, either online or in person.

First we identify where we are and where we want to go. What is our short summary of what this design is and what it is for. We have a lot of fun figuring out the name. People throw out two-word combinations for a little while, and then we rearrange the two-word combinations and invariably find a really exciting name. Now everybody is totally tuned into what we are doing and why.

Online I have a template for the 12-page download. When we have the name we copy and paste it with each anchor point, for example Regenerating Connection **vision**, Regenerating Connection **helps** etc. and then type all the team member names and copy and paste them under all 12. Everyone has access to the document and they just find their name and write there. One person is the timekeeper and everyone types for two minutes on each anchor point, and they don't have time to read each other's entries. When we're all done with that process, we'll take a break. And then we all take turns reading what we wrote, in the order that's on the document, so there's not even any thinking about who goes next, that just flows.

Invariably, what we all are continuously surprised by is how all the voices paint a consistent, unified picture. It's not like Bob was in conflict with Mary; they were literally describing two sides of the same thing. It's the same as the idea that if we all sit in a circle around a deer, the person who's looking at the face is going to see one thing. The person who's looking at the flank on the right side will describe a different view. But it's very clear by the time this process is over, which takes maybe 45 minutes in total, everyone is describing the same thing from their vantage point, from their unique perceptions and experience. It creates team unity very quickly, and roles naturally flow right out of it, and people are ready to move into action pretty quickly. It's astounding. Now whenever we feel stuck, scratching our heads or going round in circles with a particular project or part of the bigger overall aims, we turn to the Design Web.

Encouraging conversations

There are also many opportunities for us to bring design thinking informally. You can use it to support people without ever having to mention Design Web, Cultural Emergence or permaculture initially, although they might want to learn more later.

The Design Web can form the basis of encouraging conversations, where you weave this thinking as a way of supporting and guiding. When listening we might recognise when anchor points naturally appear. We can follow this with questions and guide people to other ones that they haven't yet considered. For example, someone is sharing about their lack of time/money/confidence and you hear them as their **limits**, you can then invite them to flip these around and see them as needs that they might be able to build. You might recognise a **pattern** from previously in the conversation, or from the last time you spoke.

With your children, you won't necessarily want to say to them 'let's do a design about this' but you might want to guide them through certain ways of thinking about things. Designing by stealth!

When we were trying to decide whether it was the right time to get a kitten when seeing a litter advertised locally, after going round in circles, Chris and I spoke to our daughter around the kitchen table using the Design Web cards of the CEED deck. We didn't actually want to say to her that we had seen some locally as we knew there would be no going back. Her reply to most of the questions was 'kitten'. However, it did help us to clarify that now was indeed a good moment, and to set some agreements about kitten care, and what we needed to do to prepare. The golden question that unlocked the decision came with asking Chris, "Do you want to meet the kittens before you go away to Nepal?" The design worked so well that within a week we had two kittens!

Use the intelligence of cooperating hearts

Holistic family wayfinding – Skye Jin, South Korea/Denmark

As a mother and adoptee, I have always been reading patterns: of other people's needs, of different cultures and social norms. It is like a new continent with no infrastructure yet, and can be an experience most people feel when having different values or beliefs than the majority or just other generations. Where to go now? You have to envision and reinvent new patterns for yourself and your family.

When I did my Permaculture Diploma, I realised that it was a life changing process coming from deep within my own life, my internal landscape, my own livelihood and from becoming a mother and suddenly designing life for someone else. Later on even for two children.

Like an inspiring conversation that flows with intuition, the cyclical, flexible and movable anchor points of the Design Web have become gentle, wise and trusted friends that guide me and my family through life: designs for our week, our grocery shopping, transportation, how to complete a task, my social media presence, our family vacations or a good play date.

As my children have grown older, I have involved them in mind mapping and eventually drawing the 12 symbols of the Design Web to plan weekends or family days with their friends and cousins. We are all very visual and multidimensional people in our family, so linear frameworks have rarely been the go-to for everyday quick decisions.

Quick designs are helping me to harvest fruits of previous experience, giving me direction in the preparations for an upcoming presentation or taking the temperature of my well being. By now I have designs in every notebook, on the back of receipts lying around the house and in big stacks in my studio and bedroom.

I do them on a piece of paper, usually drawn up and written up in 30 minutes, and I am always sure to get a more insightful answer of some kind, or the conclusion, that the scale needs adjustment, maybe it has to be four smaller ones instead of one big. This is crucial in maintaining the motivation to actually take action on them or tweak them.

This year we designed our vacation together as a family. Everyone is heard in the survey phase, from Noah (4 years old), Julian (10 years old) and grown-ups, Mikkel and I. Besides expressing our wishes like: I want to play with Transformers, we also ask the ethics and a few principles for advice. Of course, this leads to new insights straight away.

Julian and Noah like building, me and my partner Mikkel like permaculture and learning, so we planned to go on an exciting cob building course all of us together. It was unfortunately delayed because all of us got sick and left us a little disappointed.

So we asked the question: how can we dial back a bit and let the three ethics guide us to enjoy the rest of our vacation?

We then chose to go on vacation close to the sea and practise swimming (confidence and people care for the children), Earth care of having a local holiday in Denmark and visiting beloved friends on the way to the sea, hiking in the beautiful landscape of their town and having lots of fair shares with our children, enjoying just the natural elements, playing together in the sandy dunes and the ocean and running in the hills, laughing until our cheeks were as red as apples.

Emergence happens in relationship

Teaching the Design Web

Once you discover the wonders and effectiveness of Design Web you might be enthused to teach it to others. It is a tool in your toolbox to share with others so that it can be a tool in theirs too.

You might have specific opportunities to do this: teaching in schools, weaving it into another subject, teaching it as a tool to support relevant subjects, teaching Design Web workshops. I know that the more people that share it, the more we empower people to co-create the regenerative cultures needed to move us towards the ethics, Earth care, people care and fair shares. Each of you will be able to reach many more people than I can alone.

If you are already teaching children and young people, you might want to bring it into your existing classes, such as encouraging students to do a microgreen design for their first week at the beginning of term, a deeper one for revision, or for finding their next steps in life. One of the challenges of bringing Design Web into schools, is that it doesn't neatly fall into a category such as a tool for careers, or for mental health – it can do both and much more. I wildly envision a time where it is taught in all schools as a tool for life.

If you are teaching adults any skill, such as learning a language or a craft, you can use the Design Web as a tool for them to embed their learning, creating a plan for expanding their learning or their next craft project.

When teaching a relevant subject, such as permaculture, group skills, horticulture, project management and personal development, the Design Web becomes part of their toolkit.

If you are wanting to teach workshops specifically on the Design Web then I have both in-person and online trainings to empower you on your Cultural Emergence facilitation journey with skills, confidence and community of practice.

Some of the things to remember when teaching it are very similar to the guidelines for learning it yourself. Start small with tangible boundaries. Use tools that engage body wisdom, creativity and nature connection. Encourage looking below the surface at hidden **patterns** and **limits**. Reflect on the process, so that people expand their thinking to other designs. Share your own stories and reflections on the process.

Coaching using the Design Web

The Design Web is a fantastic framework in formal coaching settings. It is a tool for reading the inner landscape with the coach as a guide through the anchor points. The aim is to empower the person to find their own answers.

An interactive way is to lay out cards for each of the anchor points and invite the client to move to where they are called. If online this can be adapted. From what emerges in each anchor point, either the coach or the client can choose where to go next with what seems a natural follow-on. The coach is inviting the client's wisdom to flow through, instead of giving answers they are giving questions, to shine a light on their blindspots, blockages to be released, dormant visions to be reignited. The coach stretches the edges of curiosity and possibilities with their prompts. Coaching is the art of asking empowering questions.

There may be designs within designs. Some of these may be boundaried, micro-green ones, others more open-ended root ones. Some of the topics might be figuring out what is next for them, making a career change, letting go of limiting beliefs, starting a business, surfacing their gifts, giving up an addiction, nurturing their relationships. One of the aims of the coaching is to encourage them to plan more adventures for themselves, as well as while being supported.

The process becomes a dance between the anchor points. It goes beyond words when bringing the multiple intelligences into the questions and activities. Multiple intelligences is a model developed by Howard Gardner, who recognised that modern IQ tests focus only on specific intelligences and he saw that there are many more ways in which we have talents, skills and intelligences.

For each of the multiple intelligences below there are ideas of questions that activate that intelligence within us. They can be adapted to any of the anchor points.

Body intelligence – What do you notice in your body?
What movements or shapes does your body want to make to represent your **helps**?
Attach a body movement or gesture to a **vision**, so that in the future when you make the gesture again it will help you reconnect with your vision.

Mathematical intelligence – **Reflection** – on a scale of 1-10 how important/challenging/easy is this to you?

Linguistic intelligence – What affirmation would support you?
Tell stories of your past, present or future.

People intelligence – If your best friend could support you now what would they do? Imagine yourself in someone else's shoes. Look at it from another person's perspective.

Self intelligence – If your future self, or yourself as a child, could respond now what would they say?
How do you feel?
Shine the light of **appreciation** on yourself.

Nature intelligence – Look to nature for **patterns**. What do you need to compost?
What seeds do you want to plant?
What needs pruning in your life?
What season do you feel your life is in at the moment?
Find an object in nature to represent the **integration** anchor point.

Musical intelligence – Is there a sound to represent what is happening for you? e.g.
What do your **limits** sound like?
What song represents **action** for you?
Create a simple melody for one of the **principles**.

Visual and spatial intelligence – Is there an image that comes to mind? A colour or texture?
Where in the room do you feel called to go that represents **pause** and **momentum** to you?
Use your non-dominant hand to draw your **ideas**.

The role of the coach is to support and listen, reflecting back, reading what isn't being said, what is being told through the body. Ask questions with curiosity and try out different possibilities: 'I wonder..' 'Does this resonate with you?' 'What do you think about ...?' 'How does this sound to you?' Each time allowing the client to refute, redirect, fine tune or elaborate.

At times invite the client to ask their own questions of the anchor points, taking some time to listen for any responses. Questions will eventually lead to answers, even if not at that moment. Through encouraging reflections and guidance we bring to life the principle HONOUR THE WISDOM WITHIN.

At the end of each coaching session take time to reflect on what the harvest is. What are their key takeaways from the session, and what are their next achievable steps?

Part of the role of the coach is to help maintain continuity between sessions. At the beginning of the next session the coach can recap what they saw happen last time, as well as catching the story of what happened afterwards. This story can be reframed by the coach with the anchor points. For example, 'Oh you hit a big **limit**', or 'wow lots of **momentum** happening there.'

Using the Design Web while coaching provides an intuitive way to surface gifts. The principle of EMBRACE POTENTIAL is supported by the coach holding and fostering the clients' potential.

Cross-cultural designing

When designing with other people there will always be some cross-cultural translation happening. What varies though is the scale of difference; which are the influential macro and micro cultures? How much are those differences affecting our approach, as well as the design itself? What are the norms, values, expectations of how we work? There are many cultural contexts that we each live within, and our project sits within: historical as well as current ones; ones close to home, and global ones. There are structural 'isms' and privileges, rules and taboos, some of which

Bridging cultural divides – Chris Evans, UK/Himalayan Permaculture Centre, Nepal

The Himalayan Permaculture Centre (HPC) is a grassroots organisation working with farmers in Western Nepal. I have been working in various iterations of this organisation for over 35 years. While our work is centred on agroecological farming, it is also integrated with work in women's health, literacy, livelihoods and capacity-building programmes, anything to improve the quality of life.

Within the overall project is a whole ecosystem of designs. Learning the Design Web has greatly helped with this, and is an ongoing process that started with translating the Design Web into Nepali. Bit by bit, anchor point by anchor point, design by design, we are going through a learning cycle of understanding context, planning, implementing and reflecting.

Having successfully demonstrated techniques and approaches to increase productivity as well as reducing costs, HPC is entering a new phase to scale up and spread out through an expansive network of demonstration and training centres, with local government collaboration and international funding. Alongside the farms we are creating farmer-trainers, or 'barefoot consultants' (BCs). BCs are women and men farmers that have successfully established agroecology and similar demonstrations on their own land and in local communities. They are given training in both design and teaching skills so they can work within and outside of the project areas.

We are finding that all of our designs need to be a bridge between the funders, international non-governmental organisations (INGO) and the grassroots villagers, which have very different cultural norms and expectations, taboos and ways of working and learning. Alongside this are the **limits** and **helps** of governmental regulations and business needs.

we will be aware of, and others that we are unaware of for ourselves, let alone each other. Intergenerational wisdom and trauma are hovering around every decision. The macro cultures of patriarchy, extractivism, colonialism and capitalism are influencing every step in some way.

It is important to recognise that most of this is happening below our conscious awareness. The principle COME INTO THE LIGHT invites us to look below the surface, and articulate cultural norms and contexts. It invites us to listen to quiet voices and understand their perspectives.

Our designs are translated back and forth between Nepali and English and also between the different cultural languages of the academic and management based funders and grassroots and practical based farmers. The funders want reports with spreadsheets and statistics, meanwhile we are working at grassroots level, often with low literacy rates. One of our BCs who has low literacy has very high practical and facilitation skills, and has internalised the design process and shown great intuition and application.

Patterns is one of the most crucial anchor points. There are both deeply embedded multi-generational patterns, such as caste and gender roles, and rapidly changing modern ones like movement and communication patterns with roads and mobile phones. There are other cultural patterns of migration, valuing of farm work, women's health and place in the home that all influence the effectiveness of our work. A key need is to work with time constraints of farmers' busy lives. The designs are collaborative between staff, experienced BCs and farmers' groups. There is a whole ecosystem of designs within the whole project, with different people taking the lead on different ones. We recently did a design for a three-day training. We had to work within the **limits** of what the INGO wanted, while balancing the needs of the farmers. There is a design for the whole programme, then ones on specific trainings, and even smaller ones for specific sessions. Reaching youth is a crucial focus and another cultural divide that we are bridging through a design for training videos and social media. Social media is a tool to help break cultural taboos and share new cultural messages, such as using washable menstrual pads (that can be made locally).

It can be challenging, emotional and frustrating at times with all these different stakeholders, and working within the environment of capitalist encroachment on indigenous cultures. We have to understand and acknowledge these limits while taking pragmatic steps in designing to achieve our vision of co-creating abundant villages.

Top tips for collaborative design

In the spirit of the principle MANY MINDS ARE BETTER THAN ONE here are the top tips harvested from the Advanced Design Course facilitated by myself, Chris Evans and Delvin Solkinson.

Establish and agree a group culture

- Prioritise process over task in the beginning
- Pay attention to both design and process in balance (which fluctuates)
- Create agreements about timings
- Define clear roles
- Set up roles by strengths and edges

Honour all wisdom

- Find your niche and expand your edge
- Participate fully, in your own way
- Everyone is a designer with a unique style and skills
- Amplify quiet voices
- Walk your talk

Respect

- Contain thoughts until your turn
- Active listening
- Self-awareness and respect for others and yourself
- It is possible to have a healthy working relationship without being friends
- Pause and perspective
- Laugh, have fun and be playful
- Celebrate often
- Practise gratitude

Let go

- Let go of attachment to outcomes
- Let go of grip
- Let go, let come
- From fixed to flow
- Keep asking questions
- Never assume
- Be curious
- Allow free flow, non-judgemental space

Meeting needs

- Be responsible for your own needs and expressing them
- Check in to see if needs are being met, for the group and individuals
- Listen to the group energy
- Have time for emotional check-ins

Reframe conflict

- Expect and accept conflict as a fertile edge
- Reframe conflict as a form of energy
- Be open to being 'wrong' or for other people to be 'wrong' and make mistakes
- Have humility and compassion
- Experimentation not perfection
- Yes, and... rather than yes, but...
- Dare to say no
- What are each person's internal stories?
- TEPEE – Tensions, Enthusiasm, Pause, Emotional check-ins, Emergence

Do the design

- Move the tools
- Schedule time slots
- Get clear on what you are trying to achieve
- Let the design inform and form the design
- Look beyond the boundaries
- Perspective shift: bird's eye view and ant's eye view
- Hold complexity while finding easy solutions
- Simplify the complex
- Listen to your intuition as well as using analysis
- 360-degree vision, use all senses and emotional centres
- Design is about intention, process, collaboration and creativity

Designing for others

- Who are we designing for?
- Consider children and future generations
- Collaborate with people, nature, toolkit, site
- Discover which edges (physical or mental) and comfort zones can be challenged or played with
- Clarify what the non-negotiables are
- Feedback is key
- Change things for the better within the context of ethics to meet needs

Part 6

Design adventure guides

In this part we will be looking at five different guides. They can be followed as shown here, or adapted to your own flow, insights and needs.

For each guide there is an overview of the different contexts, when and how to do it and the challenges. Then I take you through the 12 anchor points with questions and activities. The anchor points follow a flow that is different from going around clockwise from **vision**. It illustrates the non-linear and interconnected nature of the Design Web. Some get visited more than once. You might find a different order makes more sense to you. You can mix and match activities and questions from each of these guides with the other ones, or adapt them in any way you wish.

The five guides shared are for:

- health and well being
- creating a culture of effectiveness in your group
- an event
- land based
- a large scale conceptual, visionary design.

Honour the wisdom within – Health and well being guide

Doing this design supports you to take agency over your body and life. Taking care of our own health and well being is something that we all need to do. It supports all of our other actions in life. We might be looking at the outside world, our workplace, family, neighbourhood or wider, wanting things to change, but starting with ourselves is the place we have most influence and impact. As this is for ourselves we are able to take responsibility for the whole process, and learn most about designing.

Different contexts

We might focus on prevention, management, recovery or cure – or all of them. The design could centre on one aspect of your well being, such as your emotional or physical health. There might also be one part of your body that is in need of attention and healing. It could deal more generally with self-care routines. You might want to give attention to a particular challenge such as sleeping patterns. Often the impetus comes from hitting a limit such as an acute illness or injury.

Choose how deep and wide you go according to your design muscles and your needs. If you are at the beginning of your journey then go for something more gentle and confined, such as a microgreen design for self-care routines in the week ahead. And then build upon this slowly with subsequent ones. If you are more experienced then you might want to tackle something deeper, such as chronic back pain, or underlying beliefs behind an addiction. We can start with one place and add more later.

Challenges

Often problems in our bodies creep up on us over years, and they become our status quo and we forget that they can change. Doing this design might bring some things into focus that were previously taken for granted. This can lead us to feeling overwhelmed or guilty. Knowing that this might happen helps us to stay with the process.

This is one that can definitely expand and encompass many more things than we originally intended. Our arms are connected to our shoulders, neck and back. Our sleeping patterns are connected to our eating, work and family patterns. Our energy levels are connected to our mindsets and cultural conditioning. Our emotional health is connected to our children's well being and the state of the world. The problems exist in an endless web of connections and it is a challenge to know where to draw the boundaries and where to follow the threads of connections to discover deeper underlying issues. One solution is to see this as an ecosystem of designs. Begin with where the issue is, or what you want to improve or prevent, and if something else comes up that is going to take you too far on a tangent then add it to a page of future ideas. Of course there are times when it is necessary to go down the rabbit hole, e.g. when we realise that we have fundamental limiting beliefs that need uprooting to prevent us over working, and exhausting and injuring our body.

When and how

After you have decided what you are going to focus on, find an inspiring name that expresses the positive outcomes you would like. Start with the 12-page download, and just go for a stream of consciousness to see what comes. Then go deeper with the questions and activities below. Either follow this order, or start with the anchor points for which you wrote less on the 12 pages.

Honour the wisdom within

Questions and activities

Reflection

What is happening in your body and mind right now?
Take a few minutes to do an internal body scan; where are the tensions? Where are the places of ease?
What has been happening in the last week?
Think of both the good and the challenging things.

Vision

What is your vision of your ideal healthy self? Take a walk in nature, or sit outside, or even watch a nature documentary, or look at a house plant if you can't get outside. Focus on a healthy plant, what are the qualities of that plant that you would like to have? Vision yourself embodying and living the ethics of Earth care, people care and fair shares. What does that look like for you?

Helps

What are your motivations for making the changes? What benefits and yields might you be able to harvest?
What internal and external resources are available to support your self-care?
For each resource you identify, either within you or around you, find a physical object to represent this, perhaps leaves or something else from nature, or objects from your home. Feel the potential these resources have to help you grow and flourish.

Limits

Reflect upon what your limits are and why you might not want to change. Identify what pulls there are in directions away from your vision.
What's holding you back?
How are you limiting movement towards your vision, either by something you are doing or something you are not doing?
What emotional or other ties to the status quo do you have?
What self or cultural limiting beliefs are there?
What concerns do you have if you were to fully embody your vision? These might be about what other people will think or say about you as well as your own.

Patterns

Draw some graphs or wave patterns of the ebbs and flows of your health. Choose an appropriate timescale for this. It might be showing your energy levels and your sleeping times over the last week.

It might be showing what's happened with your stress levels and your back pain over the last year. It could be comparing your eating times and your mood throughout the day. Draw a few waves with different things over the same timeframe, either on the same image or separately. Compare these pictures.

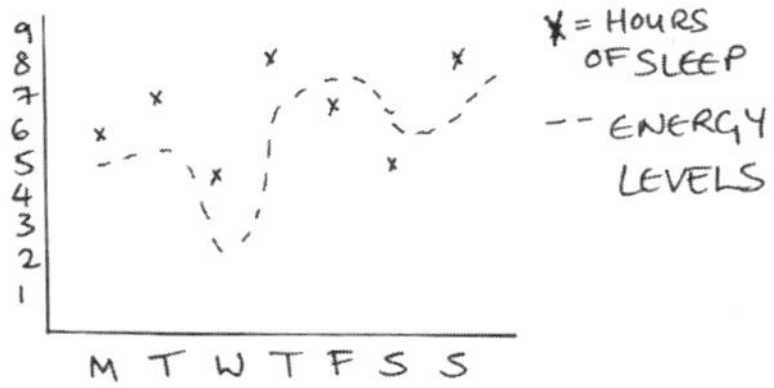

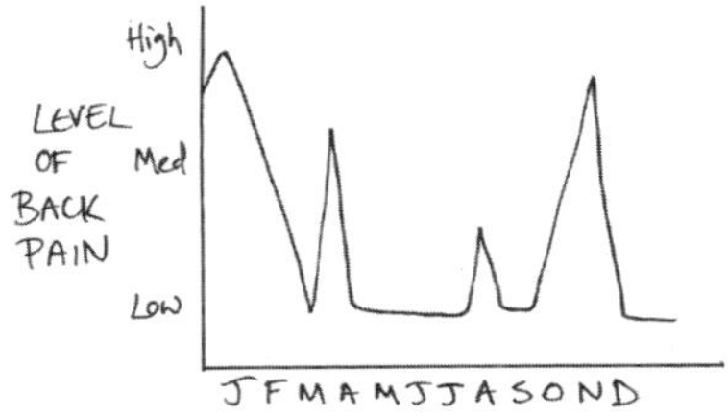

Take one of the patterns from nature (wave, branching, spiral, net) and think about how this might apply to your health.

Integration

Look at this list of functions below and choose a few that are most relevant, based on the information you have so far.

Increasing physical well being	Healthy eating
Increasing emotional well being	Increasing vitality
Increasing spiritual well being	Nature connection
Positive internal dialogue	People connection
Increasing confidence	Healing
Increasing self-esteem	Increasing stamina
Restful sleep	Strengthening body
Fun	Increasing calm
Creativity	Reducing stress
Exercising	

Exercise could be to increase flexibility, build strength, or loosen and release tension. Increasing calm and reducing stress might seem like the same thing, but each would have different strategies to meet them. Reducing stress might need a drastic fix such as changing jobs.

Ideas

Create a mind map with 'healthy me' in the middle, with the functions you have chosen coming out from it. Upon waking, put down any ideas you have for ways of meeting those needs, without censoring them. Ask your friends for ideas as well, just give them the need without giving them any story, context or **limits**. By not sharing any of your context with them, it stops them having the same constraints that you have. Ask them to be adventurous, rather than trying to be realistic with their suggestions.

Integration

Look through these **ideas** and pick out the ones that you are deciding to do. Take into account your **limits** and **helps**. Use the **principles** below to support your decision making.

Principles

If you look through the lens of each principle below, what do you see?
What does it tell you about your current state?
What ideas does it give you about the direction to go in and how to get there?
YOUR BODY KNOWS
TEND TO YOUR PERSONAL CULTURE
HONOUR THE WISDOM WITHIN
BE IN COURAGE

Action

Make a list for when you are going to implement these systems, the resources they require and the yields and benefits they will give. (You may want to use timescales of now, soon, later and long term.)

Momentum

What are the ways you can build momentum? Such as talking to friends.
What are the things that might inhibit momentum? Such as feeling guilty.
What support might you need to keep moving towards your **vision**?

Appreciation

Appreciate and thank yourself for three things that you have done this week that have contributed to your well being.
If you are focusing on one part of your body for healing, give it some appreciative attention. For example, what are all the wonderful things that your arms and hands can do?
Create a pattern of appreciating yourself at particular times of the day.

Pause

How can keeping healthy be fun for you?
How can you weave healthy habits into the whole of your life?

Integration

Draw an image to represent your design and put it somewhere you will see it everyday.

Reflections on the process

How did you feel through this process?
How did your inner designer grow?

Many minds are better than one – Creating a culture of effectiveness

This is useful for any group size. It allows you to collectively set the intention for the group. It is very much a root design, anchoring and supporting the work of the group. With an extended root system there will be new growth. We could consider that any time there is more than one person it is a group. It works for partnerships, community groups, workplaces, families.

This is a way of seeing the evolution of the group as an adventure. Being pro-active in this is showing a commitment to upgrading the way you work collectively. It is a great way of unsticking a group. It allows for exploration of hidden dynamics of privilege, conditioning and differing work ethics without blaming.

Here we deal with the commonalities of group work, rather than looking at the specifics of the type of work you are doing. You can adapt it for your specific needs.

Different contexts

Doing this is particularly useful in times of transition, expansion or downsizing. New projects, losing or gaining staff members, reaching new audiences, moving sites, moving homes, having a baby, are all times of shifting cultures. Any time the context changes, the culture also has a time of fluidity and there is a window of opportunity for shaping it.

There may be a particular emphasis on an area or discreet projects such as marketing, turning finances around, communication, office layout, personal effectiveness, vision and mission statements. Short-term effectiveness goals, such as for this month, are a way of containing it into something manageable.

Getting started

Before starting you need to have the other people on board with doing it. People need to see the value in it, and recognise that the benefits will greatly outweigh the time and energy costs.

Everyone also needs to feel that there is a safe space in which to share their thoughts and ideas. This of course may be part of the problem that you are trying to solve. In which case this feeling of safety may need to be built over time, and in a gentle way.

Doing a microgreen design, individually or collectively, for something tangible and boundaried is a good way for the group to get familiar with the Design Web and feel the benefits before embarking on a deeper root design for the whole group's effectiveness.

As talked about in part 4, designing your design culture is a way of creating a safe space for people to contribute.

Challenges

The first challenges will be convincing everyone of its need and the differences of opinion about how much time to spend on it. Once you start there will be challenges that arise from inherent imbalances that are already woven into the group, such as hierarchies of privilege, experience, skills, or time. These will show up with how much people feel they are able to speak and contribute to the design.

Being a root design, it will be connected to all the other aspects of the group, and it might be difficult to draw the boundaries, or to prioritise doing this rather than focusing on fruit designs which are more tangible. There are many rabbit holes that the group might want to explore and find it difficult to come back from. As with all designs it is one thing to do the design, it is another to implement and then maintain it.

When and how

One of the first decisions to make is about who is going to facilitate. The main options you have are for one or two people throughout, to rotate facilitation, for the group to self-facilitate or to get an outside facilitator. Each of these have their pros and cons. If one or two people facilitate then they have an overview of the whole process, but it can be considered that they either have an unfair advantage, or that any resistance or dynamics towards these people will filter through. Rotating facilitators amongst the whole group, with each person leading one or more anchor points, helps everyone to feel ownership of the process. The potential downside is losing some of the continuity. Allowing the group as a whole to self-facilitate can work very well in already functioning groups, but there will be a tendency for existing group dynamics of subtle or overt leadership to continue. Group facilitation with a group that is experiencing difficulties is likely to exacerbate rather than resolve them. An outside facilitator is very supportive in allowing everyone else to fully participate, and giving more objective observations and guidance. However, they might miss some of the unsaid patterns and norms, and also cost money. Whichever way you go it is important that everyone feels comfortable with the decision and is willing to give it a try.

You also need to decide how much time you are going to give. Are you going to do a big burst in one go, or do it in separate sessions? Set a timeframe for the whole process, and times for revisiting.

There is an interweaving between everyone's personal culture and the culture of the whole group. Personal cultures affect the collective, and the collective culture affects the personal culture. Inviting everyone to do a personal design will yield many more insights for the collective as well as fine tuning everyone's own effectiveness.

This process works in person or online or a combination of both. If you have a space where you are able to leave up flipcharts for each of the anchor points then people are able to add it as something occurs to them. If it is online then you could have an open document to add to. In some groups, some of the anchor points could benefit from being anonymous. This could be anonymous online surveys.

If a group is just forming then these questions can be adapted to reflect upon other similar groups people have been involved in.

Questions and activities

Ideas

Start with creating a place for people to add their ideas. This could be a flipchart on the wall, or an online document. Invite people to add any ideas they already have. Encourage people to continually add during the process.

Appreciation

Take time to appreciate everyone in the group for what they do and what they bring. How can you bring appreciation into the group regularly?

Some ideas for this are starting meetings with a round of appreciation, taking time to thank someone for something they have done, having a gratitude whiteboard in the tea room, appreciating people while they are still in the group, not just when someone leaves.

Vision

What are the effects you are trying to have as a group? Within the group, and in the world.
What are you trying to grow?
Do you have a vision and mission statement? If not then this is a good action point, or further design.
From your vision, brainstorm a motivating name for this design.

Integration and Reflection

For each of the following needs, ask everyone to rate them on a scale of 1-10 for how well they feel they are being effective in the group. This could be an online survey or spreadsheet, or individual papers, or collaborative paper. (Take out any that aren't appropriate for your group, and add any more that come up.)

Internal needs within the group:

Personal effectiveness
Scheduling
Communication flows
Decision making
Planning
Commitment

Learning new skills
Effective meetings
Clear group culture
Clarity of roles and responsibilities
Improving weaknesses
Connection in group
Learning and increasing design skills
Visioning
Conflict resolution
Working to strengths
Challenging and stretching edges
Fun and enjoyment of being in the group

External – interfacing with the world:

Marketing
Connecting with customers/audience
Raising awareness
Income generation
Networking with other organisations
Participation and engagement
Contributing to the ethics of Earth care, people care and fair shares

From this scaling you can then work out the average scores: 8-10 well done, 5-7 could have small improvements to streamline, below 5 needs attention.

If you have many needs, choose around three to five to work on first. Choose some to streamline for quick wins and others that need more work. As you go through the other anchor points, keep these in mind.

Helps

What can you learn from each other's effectiveness? What are the helpful patterns of effectiveness in other areas of your lives? e.g. exercising, cooking, crafting, playing music; things that other people say, 'I wish I could do that/have time/have skills'. Activities that other people don't find as effortless as you.
What do you do well as a group?

Limits

Where are the energy leaks?
For individuals – what tasks don't you like doing, and try to limit?
What are the external limits?

Patterns

What are the cultural patterns and mindsets that are influencing us?
Unhelpful patterns might include scarcity thinking, 24/7, glorification of busyness, profit over people and planet.
Helpful patterns might include planning, lists, meetings, flexibility or structure, timekeeping, data collection.

Principles

Some favourite Cultural Emergence principles that support effectiveness are
MAKE PROGRESS VISIBLE
WORK TO COMPLETION

PLAN THEN FLOW
BE ATTENTIVE TO TIMING
MOVE THE TOOLS
Ask everyone to choose a principle and how they think it will support the group's effectiveness.

Is there a group motto or principle for effectiveness?
Some of the other ones I use for keeping myself on track are:
Don't rush, but don't dither or get distracted (for timekeeping)
Be ahead of time
Productive procrastination (for when a change of task is needed)
Post before scroll (for social media)

Momentum and Patterns

At any point in time we are either increasing or decreasing in momentum and effectiveness. This can be very subtle or big momentum swings.
Plot daily and weekly and monthly patterns to see when there are dips of effectiveness that need a different activity.

Pause

What are the ways the group can connect and have fun together?
Both while working and outside of work. Examples are shared lunches once a week, bring a cake mornings, walking in nature meetings, sitting outside to work.

Ideas

Brainstorm ideas for each of the needs you want to work on and any others that have come up.

Integration

Bring back any ideas that seem currently achievable. Make a visual, table, graphic, flow diagram or post it chart showing the needs and the strategies for meeting them.

Needs	Ideas	Decisions	Action steps

Action

Keep your action plan focused on tasks for growing effectiveness, not all of the actions that the group will take. Choose a relevant timescale, such as a month with more detail in. Creating a larger action plan might be an action point in itself.

Reflection

Schedule in regular review times. In the beginning it is useful to review at the end of the first week, and the first month; after a while the reviews can become more spaced out.
Ask, what has gone well? What **limits** have we noticed?
What can we improve next?
These questions will lead you to the **appreciation**, **limits** and **action** anchor points. Other anchor points can be revisited as needed.

Reflection on the process questions

What was liberating?
What was useful and valuable to you for your own designing?
What surprised you, about yourself, about the design?
What are the dos and don'ts for designing a culture of effectiveness?

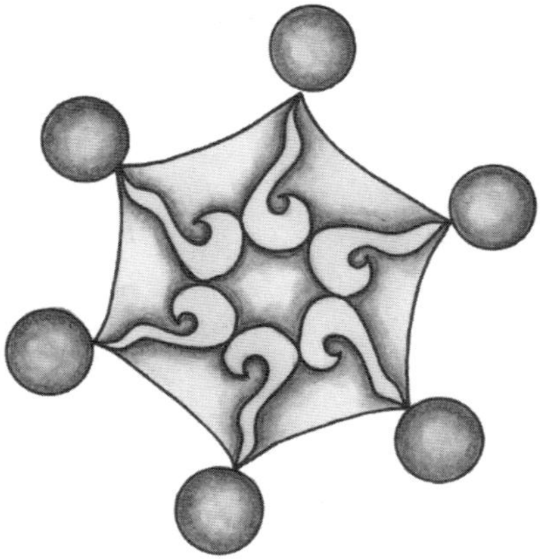

Many minds are better than one

Plan then flow – Connected events guide

This guide can be used for any event, from a course to a small gathering with friends, to a large conference. It will support you with all the planning as well as helping you navigate the event itself, to flex in the moment with emerging circumstances and needs.

This is a fruit design, it is focused on a tangible outcome. We want to get as much juice and nutrition from the event as possible.

Different contexts

These methods and questions can be adapted for any event. They can be scaled up to big events such as festivals, or scaled down to a family meal. It is good to have practice with something small like a dinner party, before doing a big gathering. Possible events might be a birthday party, fundraising event, workshop, course, talk, site visit, volunteer day, retreat, holiday, staycation, conference, Mother Nature circle, campfire, hiking trip, a community work weekend, wedding, funeral, a song circle. The events could be in person or online, one-offs or ones repeated annually, or a series of several over time. The event might be part of a whole programme of events. We have a whole programme of events at Applewood, each one is different but has many commonalities. We are able to take the overall pattern and then adapt the details each time.

Challenges

One of the biggest challenges I find with running events is the amount of thought and work that goes into them beforehand. This can be overwhelming and seem very disproportionate to the length of the event itself. On the other side of the equation though, are the benefits that events bring; some are measurable such as money, but many are non-measurable: friendships, joy, connection, purpose, skills, happiness. Events are often turning points in people's lives, leading them to people, places and parts of themselves they couldn't have found otherwise. Coming together is one of our basic needs as humans.

The other major challenge is that no amount of planning will account for all that will occur when you bring people together, their personalities, connections and needs. It is a challenge and opportunity for us as designers. We will never know how things will land with people and what will grow as a result of it. It truly is an emergent adventure.

Getting started

Sometimes the start of the process is with a collection of seeds of ideas and we need to know which one to plant. The process therefore begins with clarifying which of the options is the best one to go for. Other times we are sure what we are going to do and are ready to get on with planning it. In each scenario there is more than one threshold of commitment to cross. One of the first thresholds is when we share the event with others; we launch a webpage or send out invitations. Other thresholds come when we have ordered food, paid deposits or participants have booked travel. Sometimes these thresholds are together, often though one or more are closer to the event.

When and how

There are three phases for an event.

1. The planning phase; this goes from the seed of the idea all the way through to when people arrive.
2. This second phase is the dynamic, living design that involves everyone (even if they are unaware of it, they will be contributing to the evolution of it). People go from being just numbers of guests to individuals with their own unique needs and inputs.
3. Then there is the post-event reflective phase. This leads on to the next time, and plants the seeds for future events. This phase is often skipped or condensed but is really important for harvesting learning for the future.

There can be overlapping of these phases, such as information on booking forms, where information from the participants informs the planning and visioning. Reflections during the event may already be giving ideas for the future.

Often the planning of events happens over numerous meetings rather than all in one go. Visit some of the anchor points on each occasion, and have an iterative approach to each one. It is useful to have done a 12-page download to start with and have these pages available (possibly online) for people to add their thoughts and progress. As always, many of them connect with each other.

Questions and activities in the planning stage

Integration

Ask yourself why are you hosting this event. Look at this list of functions for an event and see which ones apply, and if there are any others to add.

Celebrating	Sharing skills
Connecting with other people	Raising awareness of an issue
Fun	Campaigning
Self-care	Learning
Connecting with nature	Collaborative work
Generating income	Collective discovery
Fundraising	Sharing best practices
Networking	Cross pollinating ideas

Ideas

If you are still unsure about the event you are running then think of all the different ways you could meet these needs. This can be within the context of the event, and is also a good moment to think of ways of meeting the need in a different way. We might, for example, assume that the best way to celebrate our birthday is with a party, but then we might see an idea of travelling to visit a long lost friend as a more nourishing way to celebrate.

A fantastic tool for generating ideas and getting us thinking outside the box is the Morphological Matrix by Tony Buzan. For this you think of three different variables, such as length of event, people and place, or dress code, activities and food for a party. For each of these variables write as many options on small pieces of paper (they could be colour coded for each variable). Then pick one from each variable at random and see how they combine, such as a week with business leaders in the Bahamas, or pirate outfits at a disco with fondue. From lots of wild combinations, a few real possibilities may arise.

Limits

Consider people's limits for attending the event. This could be time of day or year, childcare, mobility, cost, distance to travel, school holidays, language, feelings of being welcomed or not.

What are the boundaries you need to put in place? Such as dietary restrictions, late night music, length of the event, or private areas at the venue.

Use the ethics as a guide for the boundaries. What do you need to limit that is not in line with the ethics?

Reflection

Have you or any of your team attended or run similar events? What worked well? What was challenging?

Helps

Think of the experiential capital of you and your team from other events you have run in the past. What skills did you use to make it happen?

Everyone coming to the event is going to contribute in one way or another, just by being there (whether consciously or not). You can ask in advance for contributions and set the culture of fair shares and everyone contributing, such as letting people know that everyone will be helping with washing up, or by scheduling an hour of collective tidying up on the timetable before departures.

Who is coming to the event and what are they bringing? This might be tangible things, like asking everyone to bring some food to share, or some aspect of themselves that they are able to share, like their friendliness, listening, or jokes.

Action

If you haven't already done so, now is a good time to cross the threshold of commitment. What do you need to decide upon and do in order to cross the threshold? When will you take these actions? Who will do them? Do a timeline of actions between now and crossing the threshold.

Vision

Imagine yourself at the end of the event (maybe the following day). You have a smile on your face and a warmth in your heart from a satisfying event. Take time to imagine the event and the qualities of it. Put yourself in the place of someone attending: How are they feeling? What are they taking away from it?
How might this event contribute to the ethics of Earth care, people care, and fair shares?

Integration and Action

The functions above were about what to get out of the event itself. There is another group of functions for the planning of the event, such as marketing or finding a venue. These functions then take you into action.

What are the steps you need to take for each of these functions to organise the event? Put each task on a small piece of paper. Then arrange the tasks in the sequence they need doing. For example, you can't cook the food before you have bought it, or take bookings for a workshop before you have fixed the costs.

Momentum

Think about how you will pace yourself before and during the event. Some preparation tasks, such as marketing and social media, require regular inputs. What are the regular jobs during the event that will keep the place and people happy?

Patterns

What are the flows of the event? A birthday party for children will have a different flow from a weekend workshop; each one will have an archetypal flow.

In the simplest terms all events will have a beginning, middle and end, and there is also the pre-event and post-event. What are the qualities of each stage and what needs to happen at each time? In the beginning, people need to feel welcomed, there is orientation to the place, each other and the event itself. The culture of the event is being formed at this time; how explicitly this is done will depend on the context. The middle will have more flow and momentum. There is more spontaneity and emergence as people will be bringing unexpected conversations, play, questions, ideas. The end brings all sorts of other things: relief, tears, sadness, ideas for the future, tiredness, disengagement, satisfaction, joy, friendships, commitment to actions.

Take time to map the pattern of your event; this might be a daily rhythm for a course.

The event itself will be a PATTERN DISRUPTION for most people, a step away from their usual activities. So there is an opportunity to bring in new patterns.

Principles

These principles are particularly useful for events.

These ones help us to trust, flow, and not be too rigid with our plans.

PLAN THEN FLOW
LEAVE SPACE FOR EMERGENCE
RESPOND TO LIFE
TRUST THE PROCESS
BE ATTENTIVE TO TIMING

The following principles remind us that a key aim of most events is to bring people together, for support, connection and creativity. There is more that happens with a group of people than can happen alone.

MAKE CONNECTION FIRST
EMERGENCE HAPPENS IN RELATIONSHIP
USE THE INTELLIGENCE OF CO-OPERATING HEARTS
GIVE ENCOURAGEMENT
RECEIVE ENCOURAGEMENT
MANY MINDS ARE BETTER THAN ONE

Appreciation

During the planning stages, continually make time to appreciate each of the team members and the support in making the event happen.

For the event itself, plan in some opportunities for appreciation, for example: meal appreciations, introductions with your name and something you are grateful for beginning with the same letter, or something you noticed about nature on your travels, or written or spoken appreciation of each other at the end. Make the appreciation appropriate and edge stretching, a bit more than people are used to, but not so much that it is too uncomfortable.

Pause

Some events are predominately about this, with fun and connection being the key functions. For other events this is a side benefit, and needs more thought and attention of how to maximise it. How can learning be made fun, creative and embodied?

When are the break times, moments of silence, self-care opportunities, social times, nature connection moments?

During the event

Once the event has started you are in the second living, dynamic phase. You will now be continuing to visit the anchor points, either explicitly or informally. How much the design is shared with people is very context specific. On a course it is a learning opportunity to share how it is underpinning the experience, and involve people explicitly, giving them some ownership. This is not so relevant or appropriate for a barbecue with neighbours. However it is shared; people are living and dynamic components.

You can guide people through an activity to share their **vision** for the event, in terms of hopes or intentions. Their concerns are **limits** to work around, and what they bring are **helps**. Each person will be bringing their personal culture with them, including their **patterns** of interacting with each other. With their personal culture they might bring songs to share around the fire or their morning yoga practice. A suggestion box is a way of harvesting **ideas** from everyone. You could invite everyone to pick a card from the CEED deck or colour in a **principle** that they want to bring into the group culture. **Reflection** can be done informally or formally. There will be informal vibes watching (what or who needs attending to), observing who is looking distracted, bored or not participating, who is flourishing? It might be appropriate to have a structured mid-event reflection session, or ongoing feedback.

As designers you need to be observant of what is unfolding. Having the anchor points to frame this helps you to flex in the moment and ensure that you are all moving towards rather than away from your **vision**.

After the event

Asking for reflections as soon as possible afterwards gathers ideas and visions for future events. This can be informal sharing of the highlights from a workshop, or more formally with an online survey.
How will you maintain and grow the learning and connections?
Gather the seeds for next time, so you are ready to make any following events even better.

Reflections on the process questions

Which anchor points guided the process?
Which ones made the event different to how it might have otherwise been without the design?
What did you learn about collaborative designing?
What are your recommendations for designing events?

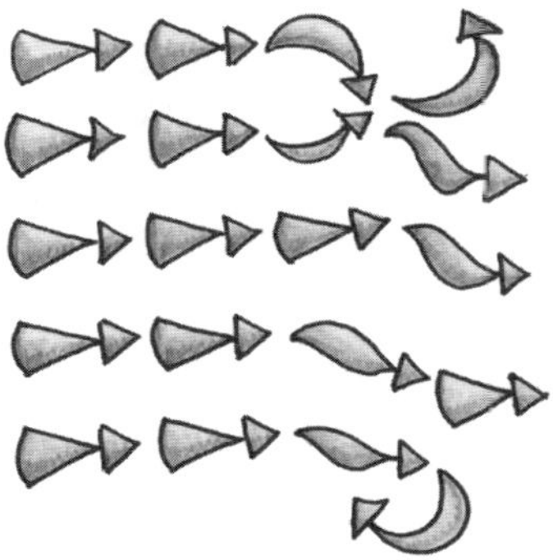

Plan the flow

Discover abundance – Land based designs

Many think that because the Design Web was created with an emphasis on people that it can't be used for land. In fact, the Design Web can be used just as effectively for land based designs as other permaculture frameworks. All land based designs are actually people based. Land without people is called 'nature getting on with it'. But even then, a plan is needed to keep people out of the area.

The Design Web invites us into partnership with the land, enhancing the ethics of Earth care, people care, and fair shares in very tangible ways.

Different contexts

There are many scales of possibility, from a small balcony to acres of farmland. Apart from the very small areas, it is appropriate to see it as literally an ecosystem of designs. Start with microgreen and seedling designs for small discreet areas or choose some themes to work on, such as water or compost. You will also want to at some point do a whole site plan that has less detail, but shows the overall areas and vision. Both going from the big picture to the detail or going from detail to big picture are useful perspectives.

Challenges

One of the challenges is that the design feels like a fixed moment in time, which has flown past by the time we get there and things have changed already.

For some of us a drawn map can seem very abstract and two dimensional compared with the multilayered reality. Rather than doing a planting plan on a map, I like to wander around with a plant and intuitively see where to plant it. But for many people it helps to decide on plants and spacing and such. It is easier to make mistakes on paper, but it is also good to check with what feels right on the land.

The process helps us to decide what we do want and don't want, giving us parameters to work within, and a direction to follow. It gives accountability and co-ownership and involvement.

Getting started

We are never starting from zero with land, every piece of Earth has been here for billions of years. How much of the story of the land we delve into depends on the context.

In other terms this is called site surveying. It is part of the **reflection** anchor point, which would also include reflections from the clients (you would be the client, if it is your garden or land).

With permaculture we are advised to observe the land for a year, to see all of the seasons before we make any big changes. In reality I think most of us can't wait to get started on small projects, although it really is a good idea to hold off making any big, permanent changes.

There are many comprehensive permaculture resources and books detailing land based tools. My aim here is to illustrate how to use the Design Web to frame the client interview to gather the information needed to integrate people and land.

At the end of any client interview there is the golden question of 'is there anything else you would like to add?' This usually elicits an important piece of the puzzle.

When and how

Take time to walk the land. It is the most appropriate time to use nature connection as a design tool. Ask the questions below of as many of the people as possible. It is good to involve everyone that is going to be using the site, including children and volunteers. After you have done the client interview you move into the next stage of analysing the information and making decisions. For placement you might want to play with cutout cards for different elements, or you could do this digitally.

Discover abundance

Questions and activities for client interviews

Reflection and Appreciation

How has the site been used in the past? By whom and when?
What do you enjoy and like about the space at the moment, or in the past?
What works well for you about the site?
What doesn't work so well for you about the site?
What do you really want to change?
In a site survey you would explore, amongst other things, the sun sectors, soil types, climate, weather, microclimates.

Draw a base map of the site with what is there at the moment.

Vision

What are your visions for the site?
What are your 'must haves'? And your 'nice to haves'?
Describe the qualities that you would like the site to have.
What are your values you would like reflected in the space?

Patterns

What are the current patterns of use?
How does the use change within the day or by season or by year?
Who uses the site, currently and expected in the future?

Helps

What material resources and utilities do you have?
What skills and knowledge do you have (for land care or otherwise)?
What time availability do you have?
What money do you have for implementation?

Limits

What are your personal limits for implementation and maintenance?
What are the site limits? e.g. soil, water, slope, aspect, wildlife, pests, etc.
Are there any other restrictions on use? Personal aversions or dislikes worth mentioning?
What are the potential catastrophes or risks? e.g. drought, fire, wind, flood?
Are there any regulations or things you need permission for?

Integration

Which of the following needs are being met, and how?
What needs are currently not being met that you would like? Or could be met more fully.

Are there other needs for the site you would like to include?

- Food production
- Increasing soil fertility
- Increasing biodiversity
- Creating wildlife habitats
- Protecting habitat
- Composting
- Waste management
- Beauty
- Relaxation
- Space for games
- Firewood production
- Grazing areas
- Growing medicinal plants
- Generating income
- Nature connection
- Education
- Demonstration
- Experimentation

Ideas

What ideas have you got for the space?
Do you have any ideas of ways to meet these needs?

Action

What is your timescale for implementation?
What are your priorities for implementing?

Momentum

How much time, energy and money in different seasons do you have available to maintain these systems?

Pause

Are there any fun, rejuvenating, restful things you would like to include?

Moving from client interview into designing

Principles

Some relevant principles

HONOUR THE WISDOM WITHIN – Tap into the wisdom of the land

MOVE THE TOOLS – Literally move your gardening tools

LEAVE SPACE FOR EMERGENCE – You don't need to fill every single part of your garden, allow some space for wilderness to run free

EMERGENCE HAPPENS IN RELATIONSHIP – You are entering into relationship with the land, it is through the combination of you and nature that the design will take shape, and this could be more abundant than your wildest imagination

SYNCHRONISE WITH NATURAL PATTERNS AND CYCLES – Find your own rhythm in relationship with nature's rhythms

EMBRACE POTENTIAL – Growth in non-linear

RESPOND TO LIFE – Life is flowing through the plants, pay attention to the ebbs and flows

TRUST THE PROCESS – As they say, create your pond and the wildlife will come.

Integration, action and momentum

You now have the information you need (or at least the starting points of it) to distil and weave it into a design.

Now work through clarifying your needs, choosing appropriate systems to meet those needs, and then working on placement. For example, you might want to produce food; there are many options of systems that could meet that need, such as raised beds, polytunnels or forest gardens, with a whole variety of possible food crops. Choose according to the information you have gathered in **helps**, **limits**, **action** and elsewhere. A polytunnel might seem like the best option. Then you would decide where to put your polytunnel, and how each system relates to each other. Bring together your design on a map.

From this you create an **action** plan, detailing when things will happen, the sequence of events, who will do them, how long things will take and what resources you need. In **momentum** you would work out what needs doing on a daily, weekly, seasonal and annual basis. There will be some back and forth between **integration**, **action** and **momentum**, while keeping in mind **helps** and **limits**, as you realise that perhaps you are being too ambitious and need to be more realistic.

Observation is key throughout; what is happening on the land? What happens at different times of day and seasons? Let nature guide you. It is not just the people that are the clients, the land is also a client. Listen to what the land is telling you, what the energy of different places is. Use your intuition and your own embodied, sensory perception to determine what feels like the right place.

Gardens are constantly growing and evolving and we never 'complete' it as such, but we can complete certain cycles and designs within the larger designs. As the garden grows we are in a constant state of **reflection** and adaptation, as well as hopefully **appreciation** for ourselves and all that is happening on the land.

Reflections on the process

When did you feel it coming into a cohesive whole?
How did your inner designer grow?
Which anchor points gave you golden keys to unlock your design?

Allow for the possibility of the seemingly impossible – Large scale conceptual visionary design

This is about stretching our imagination into the possibilities of a harmonious world. It is about allowing for the possibility of solving seemingly impossible problems. What are the really large, global entrenched issues that seem like they will never change?

It might seem absurd or a waste of time to even think about a design to prevent wars, end sexual violence, eradicate poverty, stop ecocide, bring clean water to everyone on the planet, move towards climate stability, but these are very real concerns and challenges that we are facing collectively and we need to collectively find solutions to continue to live, let alone thrive on Earth. Doing this visionary thinking stretches our imagination to a place where we have solved these problems, or at least are in the process of solving. The world is awash with films and books with imagined dystopian futures, thousands of images of how the civilisation collapses, but hardly any utopian ones. Countless hours and resources have been spent crafting dystopian stories; let's spend as long dreaming into a beautiful future, and see how it brings us hope, empowerment and action. Rupert Read and Manda Scott have coined the phrase Thrutopian: 'clear, engaging routes through to a world we'd all be proud to bequeath to future generations'. I think that the more of us that fill design library shelves with these visionary pathways, the more likely they will seed and grow into reality, although probably in unexpected ways.

Different contexts

You might choose to focus on one particular issue, or to focus on the bigger picture. There could be a local issue or more global, specific or general ones.

Challenges

There is plenty of scope here for disempowering thoughts such as 'why bother', 'doesn't matter what we do, governments, corporations, people... will never change'. Our internal cynic will convince us that it's too big and overwhelming. There will be plenty of external cynics as well, telling us it is a waste of time.

The aim however is to empower us, to give us a sense of hope, possibility and purpose. So try and redirect these negative thoughts, and say to yourself, I am learning about design, if I have just one insight or if I share just one inspiring thought with one person it will be worth it. There is a balance to be found, we do need to allow grief, sadness and anger at the state of the world to be felt and expressed, and to use these feelings to find our courage and determination to change things. Let the design work its magic and show you things that you might not otherwise see, feel or imagine.

When and how

You might like to do this whole process in one afternoon, or take time and do it over many weeks. Whatever suits you. It is great support if you have someone you can explore and journey with.

Questions and activities

Appreciation

Take time to sit in nature, sitting on the Earth if possible. Move into a space of deep appreciation, taking your awareness in layers from the sky to the rocks deep within Mother Earth. Begin with the sky, stars, sun, moon, the birds in the sky, wind and rain, move to all the land beings: the trees, plants, animals, insects, the water moving through the rivers into the seas. Next take your awareness to the soil and all the underground beings, going deeper and deeper into the Earth.

With this level of deep appreciation think of people and the wonderful beings we are; our creativity, imagination, care, productivity. Fully appreciate our human capabilities and skills.

Tune in and see if there is a poem or song or drawing, calling you from these deep appreciations.

How can you find ways to bring appreciation into your everyday interactions with people on the streets?

Vision

'The Cultural Emergence vision is to accelerate global cultural transformation towards a peaceful connected world to bring people and planet into alignment for a positive regenerative future.' Do you have your own way of expressing your vision?

Imagine getting into a time machine that is taking you to a future where this vision of a peaceful, connected world has manifested. A world where the ethics of Earth care, people care and fair shares are fully embodied and lived. Set the future date for 100 years.

Open the doors of the time machine and step into this future; you are meeting with your great, great grandchildren. Ask them to describe the world that they live in. Ask them if they have a message or gift for you to take back.

(If doing this in a group you can bring in some playful time machine sounds and movements.)

Helps

There is growing awareness of the urgency for change; this is motivation for change. What are the resources available to us to support change? Such as global communications, networks, technologies, media.
What skills do you have?

Limits

Why is it not happening? What are the cultural norms that are keeping us from moving towards the ethics? Such as greed, corruption, lack of belief, lack of care, lack of education, denial, lack of connection, disillusionment.
What are the needs that arise from flipping these limits?

Patterns

Cultural paradigm shifts are needed, otherwise proposed technological or political solutions will just reinforce the same paradigms of extractive, industrial culture.
What are the unhelpful patterns of thinking that perpetuate the problems?
What are the patterns from nature that we can translate to shift our thinking patterns to find solutions?

Integration

Let's look at the needs in the context of the ethics. What do we need to do to grow each of the ethics? Here are some suggestions, you will have others depending on the issue you are focusing on. Are there other needs from the flipped limits, or other anchor points? What are the needs that you identify as important?

Earth care

- Protecting habitat
- Cleaning water and air and soil
- Healthy food production
- Stopping pollution
- Increasing biodiversity

People care

- Cross-cultural understanding
- Empowerment
- Raising awareness
- Growing belief
- Leadership
- Peace making
- Connection
- Education
- Healthcare
- Shifting priorities
- Community building
- Governance – laws and policies
- Listening

Fair shares

- Levelling privilege
- Reparations
- Reinvesting surplus
- Amplifying voices of marginalised groups
- Reducing consumption
- Regenerative feminine leadership

Ideas

Ask friends and family, in person and on social media, what ideas are there for ways to solve the current challenges and to meet these needs – either choosing one or more issues, or asking more broadly. Invite them to be expansive. Think of one of those conversations where you put the world to rights over a cup of tea. Or take your imagination further and see yourself as a wizard able to wave your magical wand and transform things in an instant.

Principles

These principles are relevant to this large scale:

ALLOW FOR THE POSSIBILITY OF THE SEEMINGLY IMPOSSIBLE

EMBRACE POTENTIAL

BE IN COURAGE

USE THE INTELLIGENCE OF CO-OPERATING HEARTS

Action

Make a 1, 5, 10, 20 year action plan, whatever timescales you wish to work on. Do this as if there were no limits on money or political will, as if all resources were available to us for massive Earth care, people care and fair shares.
What are the small achievable steps we could take now?

Momentum

What are the ways we can increase momentum for positive actions?
How can we decrease momentum of destructive ways? What ways can we deescalate conflicts, stop erosion, hold back deforestation etc.?

Reflection

Take time to research the context of big historical changes, such as the end of apartheid, slavery. Read stories about courageous people in history.

Pause

How can we nourish and empower others?
How can we have fun and bring creativity in?

Vision

Let's come back to ourselves.
What is your mission statement? What is yours to do?

Reflection on the process

Which anchor points were most surprising?
Which ones were most challenging?
What made you smile?
What did you learn about designing?
How can you share your design with others?

Allow for the possibility of the seemingly impossible

Part 7

Rooting yourself as a designer

Make progress visible

Let me guide you one more time. This is a root design, as you might expect from the name. It will embed the learning in your life, and support you to grow and develop as a unique designer. MANIFESTING THROUGH DESIGN AND ACTION is a practice, not something we do once and then put the book on the shelf and forget about. It is something to make a healthy habit of, something to incorporate into our personal and group cultures. This will support you to make designing second nature to you.

Reflection

Take some time to look back over the journey you have been on.
What have you learnt about yourself? How have you grown and developed?
What has been challenging?

Appreciation

What amazing things can you appreciate about yourself and your inner designer?

Vision

Write an intention statement for yourself – 'I intend to become a (choose a word or two) designer', e.g. confident, embodied, collaborative, engaging, fluent, creative, inspiring, imaginative, effective. Put this on your wall.

Ideas

What ideas for designs do you have?
What ideas do you have to support your process?

Patterns

What are times of the day, week and season that reflection and planning flow for you?
What are the patterns of success from other learning experiences in your life?

Limits

What are your hesitancies? What are your blockages?

Principles

Which of these principles will support you to overcome your limits?
MAKE PROGRESS VISIBLE
BE IN COURAGE
TEND TO YOUR PERSONAL CULTURE
EMBRACE POTENTIAL
COME INTO THE LIGHT

Helps

What are the skills you are bringing?

Integration

Which of these needs are important to you?

Setting up your systems
Documenting and writing up your designs
Creating a space to design
Organising filing systems
Sharing your designs

Growing your inner designer
Building confidence
Creativity
Researching
Experimenting
Specialising
Trying new design tools

Connecting with other people
Learning from other designers
Sharing Design Web with others
Collaborating with others

Learning and practising Cultural Emergence
Learning Cultural Emergence practices
Connecting with nature
Activating and balancing CHALLENGE AND AWAKEN, MOVE AND INVIGORATE, NOURISH AND EMPOWER phases

Growing the ethics
Earth care
People care
Fair shares

Now think of the ways you can meet those needs. Some ideas are courses, books, exploring the online design library.

Action

What designs do you want to do over the coming year? Map them out on a timeline.

Momentum

Do a microgreen design each week for a month to build momentum.
Then try a seedling one, and expand from there.
How are you going to keep going?
What strategies can you put in place for support?

Reflection

Book time in your calendar now for monthly reviews. Ask yourself what are the ways designing has supported me? What challenges have I overcome? What challenges have I got a bit lost in?

Appreciation

Each time you start a design session, take some time to appreciate yourself. At the end take a moment to appreciate progress.
What can you do to celebrate your successes and efforts?

Pause

How does designing relax you?
What ways of designing energise you?
How can you get started again after a pause?

Reflections on the process

How does this design show my growth as a designer?
How has my understanding of designing, the Design Web and the anchor points grown?
What are my best practices?
What would I recommend to someone just starting their journey?

Design adventurer

Earth repairer
Ethics grower
Life protector
Vision believer
Helps mapper
Limit flipper
Pattern disruptor
Ideas illuminator
Principle translator
Integration weaver
Action manifester
Momentum builder
Appreciation bringer
Reflection analyser
Pause regenerator
Paradigm shaker
Cultural emerger
Unboundaried dreamer
Progress tracker
Health nourisher
People connector
Edge dweller
Dream inspirer
Flow planner
Abundance creator
Co-operation observer
Nature collaborator
System sensor
Quantum leaper
Future carer
Solution finder
Design adventurer

Beauty in completion

A spider starts its web by releasing multiple threads of silk, and then waits for the slightest breeze to catch one. The wind carries it off and it finds a branch or fence post, blade of grass or doorframe, wherever it lands this becomes the first anchor point. From this the spider begins to weave its web. The spider finds more anchor points, weaving radial branches, and the sticky capture spiral, sometimes doubling back on itself to create the perfect balance and tension. They pause while creating the web. They adjust their weave depending on what they want to catch. And when ready the spider patiently waits. They don't know when they will catch their prey but they know they are ready when the opportunity flies by.

What webs are you going to weave?

The end makes sense of the beginning. Here we are at the end of this journey together, but it also marks the beginnings of a new chapter. What do you feel inspired to continue? What are your wildest dreams of the best possible version of yourself you could grow into?

We don't know what is next on our individual and collective travels. There will undoubtedly be many twists and turns along the way. No one can deny that we are living in uncertain times, with multiple complex challenges facing us. What is also undeniable though is that humanity is resourceful and creative. Collectively we have the resources needed to grow the ethics, to weave new culture, to design lives of hope, joy, connection, peace and purpose. Each design we do is a contribution to the growing wave of people that are finding ways to live in harmony.

There are emergent possibilities that we cannot see at this moment, doors that will open up to us, that will enable us to make the Great Turning, to find pathways to a life sustaining culture. It is with the interweaving of all of our gifts, all of our relationships, all of our collaborations that we have the greatest potential for solutions to emerge.

It is going to take navigation, orientation, organisation and commitment to find our way to a world we are proud to leave to future generations. It will take trust and action, design and vision, hope and reflection, rest and effectiveness.

We need to see where we want to go in our minds, sensing the possibilities and longings in our hearts, leaning into our visions. Leaning into the needs of humanity, the needs of Earth. The more we align ourselves individually, the more we have a chance collectively to turn these challenges into opportunities. Together we are weaving webs of care, influence, connection, vision.

Stay involved, join the Cultural Emergence movement and share your stories, experience and insights. And together we will grow our inner designers, and collective wisdom. Keep learning, growing, sharing, evolving, discovering, weaving, designing.

Cultural Emergence principles

Principles for growing inner wisdom

HONOUR THE WISDOM WITHIN
Use body intuition when designing
All senses provide information
Every system holds wisdom
You hold the answers

YOUR BODY KNOWS
Your body knows how to be uniquely you
Ask your body and listen for the response
Follow your body radar

TEND TO YOUR PERSONAL CULTURE
Become a conscious culture creator
Weed out negative conditioning
Water healthy habits
You are a cross-pollinator between cultures

Principles for creating fields of encouragement

BE IN COURAGE
Courage is being in touch with our hearts
Being vulnerable is an ability
Reframe nervous energy as courage surfacing

GIVE ENCOURAGEMENT
Your presence is a present
Build a trusting relationship
Connect people with their own heart

RECEIVE ENCOURAGEMENT
Open ears, heart and mind to receive
Allow it to transform your self limiting beliefs
Widen the channels to receive from many sources

USE THE INTELLIGENCE OF CO-OPERATING HEARTS
Speak from your heart
Tap into a deeper level of information
Aim for the good of the whole
Align the group to common ethics and values

Principles for strengthening co-operation

ANYONE CAN RAISE THE VIBRATION
Empower the group to explore new territory
Bring energy into the system
Release control

EMERGENCE HAPPENS IN RELATIONSHIP
Relationships create life
Identify patterns, cycles and potentials of your interactions
Add fertility to the soil of your relationships

MANY MINDS ARE BETTER THAN ONE
Create solutions for everyone
Gain a diversity of perspectives
Honour the beginner's mind

WEAVE UNITY
Weaving relies on repetition, rhythm and pattern
Dynamic unity
Make connections visible

Principles for aligning

RESPOND TO LIFE
Sense shifting energies
Dance and flow
Pay attention to what is real

BE ATTENTIVE TO TIMING
Wait for the right moment
Feel the music in your body
Create agreements around timing

BE ATTENTIVE TO SHIFTS, OPENINGS AND OPPORTUNITIES
The world is forever changing, shifting and evolving
Observation is key
Follow the energy of the moment

SYNCHRONISE WITH NATURAL PATTERNS AND CYCLES
Follow your own needs
Surf the waves of waxing and waning
Notice the flows of days and seasons

Principles for inviting flow

TRUST THE PROCESS
Lean into the methods
Articulate the process
Reflect on the ebbs and flows

STEP INTO THE UNKNOWN
Expect the unexpected
Take the first step
Expand into new ways of knowing

USE EMERGENCE TO SUPPORT EMERGENCE
Answers are revealed as stories unfold
Do what can be done now
Emergent properties provide springboards and snowballs
Ask questions that bring more questions

PLAN THEN FLOW
Plans direct attention, energy and resources
Follow energy, enthusiasm, curiosity and impulses
Ask – What is needed right now?

LEAVE SPACE FOR EMERGENCE
Invite spontaneity
_________?
Release the need for fullness

Principles for being proactive

MOVE THE TOOLS
Show up and see what emerges
Movement invites flow and release
Create a pathway for imagination to meet the material world

PRESENCE IN THE PROCESS
Gain clarity about the process
Observe what is actually happening right now
Lose attachment to outcomes

MAKE PROGRESS VISIBLE
Highlight incremental changes
Visibility increases motivation
Ask others for reflections on progress

WORK TO COMPLETION
Choose scale of completion
Chunk tasks
Celebrate achievements

BEAUTY IN COMPLETION
The end makes sense of the beginning
Energy is released in completion
A new whole comes into being

Principles for emerging potential

COME INTO THE LIGHT
Look below the surface
Be bold
Listen to quiet voices
Bring your gifts into the light

DISCOVER ABUNDANCE
Gratitude is a potent path of discovery
Follow curiosity
Discover many ways of knowing

EMBRACE POTENTIAL

Potential may emerge quickly or slowly
Open your arms to possibilities
Potential is nonlinear

ALLOW FOR THE POSSIBILITY OF THE SEEMINGLY IMPOSSIBLE

Give voice to your heart's desire
Widen parameters of possibility
Stay engaged with searching for solutions

Index of design stories

Index

Essential books for design adventurers everywhere

CULTURAL EMERGENCE

Looby Macnamara

PEOPLE AND PERMACULTURE

Looby Macnamara

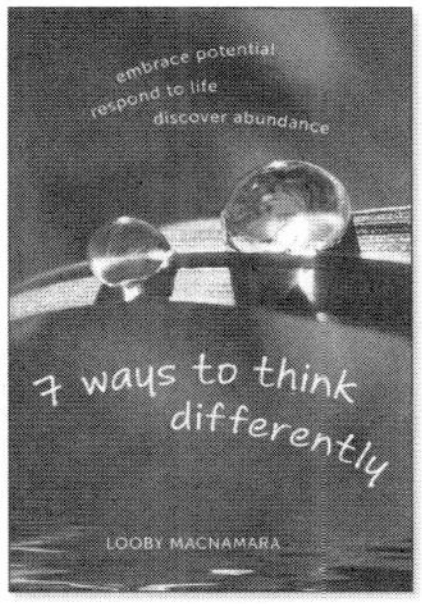

7 WAYS TO THINK DIFFERENTLY

Looby Macnamara

PERMACULTURE DESIGN: A STEP-BY-STEP GUIDE

Aranya

PERMACULTURE DESIGN COMPANION

Jasmine Dale

TRANSFORMATIVE ADAPTATION

Rupert Read and Morgan Phillip

For the full list of our solution-based titles visit
www.permanentpublications.co.uk

permanent publications
EARTH CARE, PEOPLE CARE, FUTURE CARE

Our books are also available in:

North America: https://tinyurl.com/ChelseaGreen

Australia: https://tinyurl.com/Peribo

Also available in all good books shops

Permanent Publications also publishes *Permaculture* magazine